GW00585920

MANXMAN

The 21st Century
GAME CHANGER

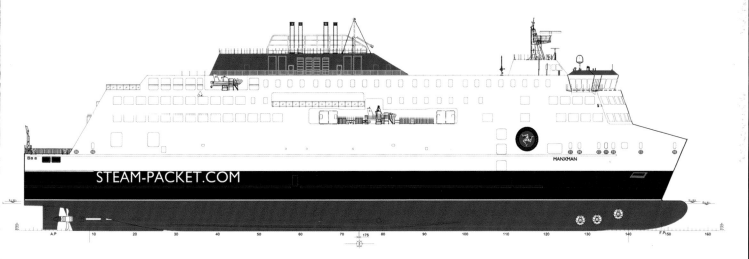

STEAM-PACKET.COM

MANXMAN

Miles Cowsill and Richard Kirkman

with Andy Atkinson, Peter Corrin, John Hendy and Jim Royston

Ferry
Publications

Published by: Ferry Publications, Ballachrink Beg, Jurby East, Ramsey IM7 3HD
Tel: +44 (0) 1624 898446   E-mail: info@lilypublications.co.uk   Website: www.ferrypubs.co.uk

John Bryant

All rights reserved

Published July 2023.

ISBN: 9781911268703

The rights of Miles Cowsill and Richard Kirkman are to be identified for this work have been asserted in accordance with the Copyright Act 1991.
No part of this publication may be reproduced, stored in a retrieval system or transmitted in any form or by any means, electronic, mechanical, photocopying,
recording or otherwise, without prior permission in writing from the publisher or the Isle of Man Steam Packet Company Ltd.

Produced in the Isle of Man by Lily Publications Ltd. Ferry Publications is a trading name of Lily Publications (IOM) Ltd.

CONTENTS

I T is the fate of islands all over the globe, that they should explore the benefits of other shores. Be it for trade, communication or just pleasure, islanders have always recognised the importance of access to their neighbours, which in turn can have reciprocal benefits.

The Isle of Man is no exception to this, and for centuries Manx people have sailed across the Irish Sea and beyond. In 1830 the Isle of Man Steam Packet Company was formed to provide passenger and freight services to England and Ireland. The company's first vessel was a wooden-hulled paddle steamer *Mona's Isle* and throughout the last 190 years the design and construction has changed enormously. Each new addition to the Company's fleet has sought to provide a better vessel than its predecessors.

In 2019 the Board of Directors of the Isle of Man Steam Packet Company began the process of building the latest addition to that fleet, *Manxman*. The concept was decided upon, and in June 2019 a brief was given to Houlder Marine to design the new ferry. 27 shipyards were contacted, 22 in Europe and five in the Far East. Out of these, 21 shipyards expressed interest, and each sent a tender document. After reviewing all of these, five shipyards were selected, four from Europe and one from the Far East.

During the spring of 2020, negotiations with these shipyards took place and in late spring this was whittled down to the final two contenders, one in Poland and one in Korea. After intense negotiations with both shipyards, it was decided to sign a Letter of Intent with Hyundai Mipo Dockyard (HMD) in South Korea. This shipyard offered the best price and with the reputation as one of the best shipyards in the world, a Shipbuilding Contract was signed on 31st July 2020.

It was impressive to observe that HMD was able to keep to the building schedule right through the pandemic. As per the Shipbuilding Contract the first milestone was steel-cutting on 20th August 2021, which took place on

that day. Then came Keel Laying on 24th December 2021, which also took place on the contractual day. Launching again was per contract on 14th June 2022. Delivery was scheduled for 30th November 2022.

However, the Board of Directors and Management made various changes to the specification and therefore the shipyard needed more time to complete the vessel. New dates were agreed, and the Isle of Man Steam Packet Company was able to take delivery as per the new delivery date of 11th May 2023.

Right from the outset of this project, the overall focus was to deliver a quality vessel for the people of the Isle of Man. The right shipyard was selected and SeaQuest, the excellent supervision company in Korea looking after the construction of the vessel, made sure the Steam Packet Company received the quality vessel that it demanded. The interior design was carried out by SMC Design, who also provided the interior design for *Queen Mary 2*, amongst many other 5-star cruise liners.

The artwork commissioned for *Manxman* has been sourced from talented artists based in the Isle of Man.

This project has been extremely challenging. However, there has been teamwork of the highest order; the Board of Directors, the Management, the Technical Department, they have all played a vital part in making *Manxman* the exceptional vessel that it is.

As Chairman of the Board of the Steam Packet Company, I would like to thank everyone involved for their hard work and dedication. Personally, I am pleased to have played a small part in the journey of *Manxman*.

Lars T Ugland
Chairman

INTRODUCTION

THE Isle of Man is dependent on the Steam Packet Company's lifeline services from Douglas to Heysham, Liverpool, Belfast, and Dublin, for the substantial freight and passenger flows that help maintain the Island as an outstanding place to live and work. The Irish Sea is an unforgiving operating environment, yet the ro-pax *Ben-my-Chree* and the high speed craft *Manannan* have consistently maintained the Steam Packet's enviable tradition of reliability and punctuality. The *Ben-my-Chree* in particular, has proved a remarkable workhorse through the last quarter century, but the need to introduce the next generation of vessel has been recognised for some time.

When the Steam Packet Company was taken into the secure ownership of the Isle of Man Government in 2018, the new vessel project was a fundamental part of the financial structure, and Tynwald soon approved the investment arrangements. The Sea Services Agreement between the Government and the Steam Packet Company helpfully provided the contractual requirements that underpinned the design and characteristics of *Manxman*.

The once-in-a-generation opportunity to design and build a new vessel for the Manx routes is one that has been enthusiastically embraced by everyone associated with the project. We have been privileged to work with a world-class team in delivering every aspect of *Manxman*, and she is a fitting legacy of the breadth of talent involved in the project. Building in Korea has proved no barrier to delivering an outstanding vessel and the Board's confidence in selecting the Hyundai Mipo shipyard has been well placed.

Marine technology has developed significantly since *Ben-my-Chree* was built, and environmental legislation is adapting to the challenges of climate change. We have therefore been able to harness new technology to ensure that *Manxman* is the most environmentally friendly vessel ever operated in the Steam Packet fleet.

It was important that the process by which *Manxman* was designed and built is permanently recorded, and that the contributions of a wide range of suppliers are acknowledged and celebrated, for this was very much a team effort united by a common goal. I am delighted to introduce this book as a lasting volume that commemorates the work of so many individuals who participated in the project.

art pieces that celebrate the Island whilst being integrated to the interior design. Each artist is profiled in this book.

Bringing greater capacity with enhanced passenger comfort and accessibility, whilst reducing fuel consumption and environmental impact, *Manxman* is a fitting flagship for the Isle of Man, and the Steam Packet Company. There is no doubt she will transform sea travel to the Island and quickly become the envy of other offshore communities around the British Isles.

It has been my privilege to lead the management team that delivered the *Manxman* project, opening the next chapter in the illustrious history of the Isle of Man Steam Packet Company.

We look forward to *Manxman* maintaining the proud traditions of the Company to the bicentenary and beyond.

The Steam Packet Company has a remarkable history and the story of previous vessels bearing the proud Manxman name is rightly recognised in these chapters. The philosophy behind the engineering and internal design of *Manxman* plays tribute to the leading designers that combined their talents to deliver a step change in quality and comfort. The process of building the vessel within strict contractual parameters by the Ulsan team remains a key element of the narrative. The extraordinary journey half way round the world to deliver *Manxman* from Korea to Douglas is recounted by Capt. Andy Atkinson.

The Isle of Man is blessed with an outstanding breadth of artistic talent, and *Manxman* hosts bespoke

Brian Thomson
Managing Director

CHAPTER ONE

THE BEN-MY-CHREE YEARS

The Isle of Man Steam Packet Company had maintained a proud record of 166 years of continuous service to the Island as an independent company but the announcement, on 29th March 1996, that Sea Containers Isle of Man owned 58% of the Company's shares, concluded a protracted and strongly contested takeover battle. Most remaining shareholders accepted Sea Containers' offer and by the 166th Annual General Meeting on 2nd May, Sea Containers controlled over 95% of the shares, leading to the Isle of Man Steam Packet Company being delisted on the Stock Exchange.

Following Sea Containers' first takeover approaches in 1990, the Steam Packet bought the popular flagship *King Orry*, refurbished *Lady of Mann*, and introduced fast craft services to the Island, despite doubts about their viability, that saw *SeaCat Isle of Man* withdrawn for the 1996 season. The freighter *Peveril* completed the Manx fleet.

The new owners sought to slim down the fleet, placing an order in early 1997 with Van der Giessen-de Noord for a new ro-pax vessel to replace the *King Orry* and *Peveril*. The 125-metre vessel, to be named *Ben-my-Chree* [6], was designed as a high-capacity freight ship, with minimal facilities for just 500 passengers. Her keel was laid down in Rotterdam on 28th October 1997.

Meanwhile Sea Containers' enthusiasm for fast craft saw the return of *SeaCat Isle of Man* on an intensive programme of sailings for summer 1997. The *Lady of Mann* opened a new Liverpool-Dublin route, with her scheduled six-and-a-half-hour passage often surpassed. The following year the *SeaCat Danmark* and *Lady of Mann* supplemented services for the TT race period before the latter sailed for the Azores on a three-month charter. The *SuperSeaCat Two* took over the Liverpool-Dublin service, although recurrent technical problems and bad weather led to *Lady of Mann* covering many services on her return from the Azores.

The new £24 million *Ben-my-Chree* arrived in Douglas from Rotterdam on 6th July 1998 and soon entered service as a freight vessel, enabling *Peveril* to be withdrawn from service. She started full passenger services on 4th August 1998, with *King Orry* retained as the back-up vessel until 29th September. The *King Orry*

Invited guests gather at the Van der Giessen-de Noord shipyard for the naming of **Ben-my-Chree**. *(Ferry Publications Library)*

The **Ben-my-Chree** lies alongside the shipyard in Rotterdam prior to departure for Douglas. *(Ferry Publications Library)*

The **King Orry** proved a popular flagship for the Steam Packet before being displaced by **Ben-my-Chree**. *(Ferry Publications Library)*

Veteran *Lady of Mann* in Sea Containers livery off the Victoria Pier, Douglas. *(Miles Cowsill)*

was quickly sold to Moby Lines. of Italy for £2 million, leaving the Mersey on 23rd October as *Moby Love*. The quality build of this former train ferry is reflected in her continued service in 2023 in Greece as *Sporades Star*, having outlived virtually all her contemporaries.

Passenger facilities on *Ben-my-Chree* received much criticism, and in October 1998 the Manx Parliament appointed a Select Committee to examine the frequency and quality of the Steam Packet's passenger services. At the end of the year, the Company announced a maximum 'comfort level' of 350 passengers for *Ben-my-Chree*.

In 1999 *SeaCat Isle of Man* returned to Manx waters, with *Lady of Mann* retained as back-up for *Ben-my-Chree* during the peak summer; later in the year she

covered fast craft cancellations on the Liverpool-Dublin and Liverpool-Douglas routes.

Six vessels were in operation for the 2000 TT: the *Ben-my-Chree*, *Lady of Mann*, *SuperSeaCat Two*, *SuperSeaCat Three*, *SeaCat Isle of Man*, and *SeaCat Scotland*. The *Lady of Mann* then sailed to the Azores for another three-month charter. She visited Cammell Laird's Birkenhead yard for a refit and SOLAS upgrade at the end of February 2001, that added a high-speed rescue craft to her starboard-side boat deck.

Foot and Mouth disease dominated 2001, forcing the cancellation of the TT Races to prevent the disease reaching the Island. The *Lady of Mann's* Irish Sea schedule was cancelled, but she again visited the Azores on a three-month charter. In early 2002 the Company agreed a five-year extension to the 'User

The *Isle of Innisfree* was built at the Van der Giessen-de Noord shipyard in 1995 as a 'stretched' version of the design later used for ***Ben-my-Chree***. *(Miles Cowsill)*

Condor Ferries' ***Commodore Clipper*** is a 1999 example of the ***Ben-my-Chree*** design, employed on the Channel island services. *(Miles Cowsill)*

A further development of the ***Ben-my-Chree*** design built at the Merwede shipyard in the Netherlands in 2005, ***Hammerodde*** is still in service as ***Stena Vinga*** for Stena Line. *(John Bryant)*

The **Ben-my-Chree** prepares to swing in the harbour at Douglas on arrival from Heysham with a well loaded sailing. *(Miles Cowsill)*

Agreement' with the Isle of Man government for the Edward Pier linkspan in Douglas. TT traffic rebounded after the previous year's cancellation, with the highest recorded figures for TT ferry traffic for over 20 years.

Sea Containers placed the Company up for sale on 24th March 2003, valuing it at £150 million. The Isle of Man government was not interested in a purchase, and Montagu Private Equity were announced as the new owners on 30th June 2003, having paid £142 million to Sea Containers. One early decision of the new owners was to initiate a £1.5 million project to add new passenger areas to *Ben-my-Chree* to accommodate her full complement of 500 passengers. The vessel returned to service in February 2004 with

an extension to her accommodation providing a new quiet lounge and bar. The forward reclining seating lounge became a First-Class lounge, matching the facilities of other ships in the fleet.

Another record TT season followed in 2004 with a variety of vessels supporting operations, including *SuperSeaCat Two* and *Rapide*. Once again, *Lady of Mann* went to the Azores on charter and returned to Irish Sea operations in late October.

The *SeaCat Isle of Man* was acquired by a new operator for the Liverpool-Dublin service in early 2005, following the Company's decision to withdraw from this route. Plans to replace *SuperSeaCat Two* came to naught with a decision put on hold following the Isle of Man government's decision to subsidise air fares to

The *SuperSeaCat Two*, later renamed *Viking*, was the vessel replaced by *Manannan* in 2008. *(Miles Cowsill)*

promote tourism, that led to a 12% reduction in sea passengers. The 2005 season was the 175th anniversary of the Company's formation, with a 'Round the Island' excursion on *Ben-my-Chree* marking the climax of the celebrations. The *Lady of Mann* was sold to SAOS Lines of Greece in September, leaving the Mersey on 22nd October, and marking the end of side-loader services on the Irish Sea.

Meanwhile, Montagu Private Equity's interest in the Company proved short lived, and in late 2005 ownership transferred to the Macquarie Bank of Sydney, Australia. Whilst the takeover had little operational impact, the Company's Douglas offices at Imperial Buildings were sold to the Isle of Man government for £8 million. There were growing concerns over the future of Island services, with proposals for a new fast craft seeming ever distant.

Six vessels were employed during the 2006 TT, but concerns were raised about the availability of vessels to accommodate the large numbers of visitors expected for the centenary TT in 2007. The *SuperSeaCat Two* suffered a main gearbox failure on 22nd July 2006, necessitating the removal of the gearbox and reduced-speed sailings throughout that summer. The *Sea Express 1* (ex *SeaCat Isle of Man*) was re-introduced on 11th September and made available to assist during the 2007 TT Race period.

Work to replace the Isle of Man linkspan at Heysham got underway during early 2007, accompanied by an upgrade to the passenger facilities at the port. The timetable featured both *SuperSeaCat Two* and *Sea Express 1* operating alongside *Ben-my-Chree*, enabling more civilised timings for Irish sailings. The *Sea Express 1* collided with the Greek bulk carrier *Alaska*

Rainbow in the River Mersey in thick fog on 3rd February 2007 and was holed below the waterline. Fortunately, no injuries were sustained on either vessel. The *SuperSeaCat Two* was already in dry dock, so *Ben-my-Chree* operated a service to the Twelve Quays terminal at Birkenhead for three weekends in March. The *Sea Express 1* was repaired, repainted, and renamed *Snaefell* but was not available until the 2008 season. The centenary TT therefore provided challenging, but some 94,000 passengers were carried over a three-week period, alongside 46,000 vehicles. Most sailings were operated by *Ben-my-Chree*, *SuperSeaCat Two*, *Emeraude France*, and *P&O Express*, with *Stena Caledonia* also chartered for two weekends.

Hamish Ross retired from the position of Managing Director at the end of June, having been in the position since 1996 when the Company was purchased by Sea Containers; the role passed to Mark Woodward. In the meantime, a Tynwald Select Committee was appointed to investigate fares and examine whether these were compliant with the User Agreement.

The *Ben-my-Chree's* sailings to Twelve Quays proved successful and a winter weekend service was introduced to Birkenhead in 2007/8.

A rebranding exercise saw *SuperSeaCat Two* renamed *Viking*, and both she and *Snaefell* appeared for the 2008 season with gloss black hulls, a bright red boot topping, a darker red funnel with wider black bands and the website address in white capital letters on the hull. The rebuilt *Snaefell* returned to service on 12th May for a TT period that saw passenger levels back to those of the 2006 festival. The *Stena Caledonia* returned for two weekends, as did *P&O Express* from Larne.

The lengthy search for a new fast craft concluded on 19th May 2008 when the Company purchased InCat's 1998-built 96-metre hull 050 to replace *Viking*. The vessel had operated initially in Australasia before being chartered to the US Military in 2001, giving her low operating hours compared to other vessels of a similar age. She left Hobart, Tasmania, on 23rd June

The **Ben-my-Chree**, now with her additonal passenger accommodation block added, backs onto the Edward Pier berth berth in Douglas as **Lady of Mann** lies at the seaward end of the Victoria Pier. *(Miles Cowsill)*

The **Emeraude France** was drafted in to provide additional services for the centenary TT races of 2007. *(Miles Cowsill)*

The **Stena Caledonia**, on one of her rare TT visits to the Island. *(Miles Cowsill)*

The dramatic livery of **Seacat Diamant** in Douglas harbour. *(Miles Cowsill)*

and arrived in Portsmouth in mid-July for an extensive refit. New accommodation modules were added, increasing her capacity from 400 passengers to over 800. The purchase price and refit cost totalled some £20 million.

Juan Kelly retired as Chairman in June 2008 and was succeeded by Robert Quayle.

A public competition saw the name *Manannan* chosen for the Incat 050. Delays were encountered with the rebuild following a cold winter, but *Manannan* arrived in Douglas on 11th May 2009. On her approach she met *Snaefell* on her way to Liverpool, before circling round *Ben-my-Chree* departing for Heysham. Her maiden voyage took place on 22nd May to Liverpool. The *Manannan* was well received, although her passenger lift proved temperamental at times.

The *Viking* was offered for sale or charter following the 2009 TT; she spent the summer in the Azores and was sold to Hellenic Lines and re-named *Hellenic Wind* in September. Although *Snaefell* began the season operating alongside *Manannan*, her future was now in doubt.

A group of local hauliers began a competing container service between Glasson Dock and Ramsey in November 2009, capturing some freight traffic. The operation later moved to Douglas to overcome tidal issues at Ramsey, but ceased in February 2011 after low growth made the service unsustainable.

The Icelandic volcanic ash cloud of April and May 2010 brought severe disruption to air traffic but benefitted the Company, with a 50% increase on normal Spring loadings. After a successful TT Festival, one of *Manannan's* Caterpillar engines suffered a serious crankshaft issue. She maintained services at reduced speed, but *Snaefell* also suffered a similar failure. The *Snaefell* was offered for sale in late 2010 and the following year was sold to Taxyploa Maritime Company and re-named *Master Jet*, reducing the Steam Packet fleet to just two vessels.

The Company announced another new ownership

The original fast craft - *SeaCat Isle of Man* initiated catamaran services to the Isle of Man in 1994. *(Miles Cowsill)*

The *Viking*, formerly *SuperSeaCat Two*, arrives in Douglas wearing the modern Steam Packet livery. *(Miles Cowsill)*

The *Ben-my-Chree* eases onto her Edward Pier berth in Douglas. *(Miles Cowsill)*

structure in April 2011, following a refinancing deal with a group of banks led by Banco Espírito Santo of Portugal.

The *Manannan* completed the 2013 season with a proud record of 100% technical reliability and 98% service reliability. Ellan Vannin Line announced plans to operate freight services to the Island from late 2013 with passenger sailings following from the 2014 TT. Chairman Robert Quayle rebuffed the concept, noting that history had proved that there was insufficient traffic to support two operators, whilst recent financial restructuring had halved debt, enabling the Company

The freighter **Arrow** has proved a useful addition to the fleet, providing service back up and charter revenues. *(Miles Cowsill)*

to consider future developments and new vessels with confidence.

Winter weather in 2013/14 disrupted *Ben-my-Chree's* services to Heysham and Birkenhead, with one storm damaging a stabiliser fin, necessitating an unscheduled visit to dry dock. The fin was severely damaged and could not be replaced until May. The freighter *Arrow* was chartered to cover the TT period and *Ben-my-Chree's* dry dock period.

Meanwhile, shares in Banco Espírito Santo were

suspended by the Bank of Portugal, just as the Company was gearing up for the 2014 Festival of Motorcycling. The Bank announced a financial restructuring to deal with its debts and there was no impact on Company operations.

Lengthy negotiations between the Steam Packet and the Isle of Man government for a new User Agreement had not reached consensus at the end of 2014 despite discussions dating back to 2010. The existing Agreement was due to expire in 2020 with a six-year optional extension, but investment by the Company was deemed unlikely without the protection of a User Agreement. The government applied pressure by requesting expressions of interest from operators who might supply sea services to the Island. Some eight operators expressed interest, which placed plans for a new Company vessel in further jeopardy. Meanwhile, the Liverpool Landing Stage was the subject of discussions between Peel Ports, the Company, and Isle of Man government as it approached the end of its useful life. The government was keen to secure long term access to the Landing Stage.

The *Manannan* suffered serious damage to her trim tabs during a sailing from Douglas to Dublin on 1st April 2015, and was out of service for ten days; the *P&O Express* and *Arrow* were drafted in to cover sailings. Bad weather and further technical problems occurred through April and May, leading to questions in Tynwald about the suitability of the Company to provide lifeline services to the Island. Silting at Heysham and bad weather continued throughout the TT Race period and into June.

On 23rd March 2016, *Manannan* collided with the Victoria Pier in Douglas whilst arriving from Liverpool; several passengers needed hospital treatment. The *Arrow* was summoned to assist, while *P&O Express* covered one sailing from Larne. The *Manannan* went to dry dock and returned to service on 3rd April. The *Arrow* remained in Manx waters to cover for *Ben-my-Chree's* biennial dry dock. The *Ben-my-*

Chree sailed to Holyhead for berthing trials as a back-up port on 21st May and *Manannan* followed on 30th June. The *Manannan* visited Larne for trials in March 2017 with *Ben-my-Chree* following in July.

The Company outlined plans for a £170m investment in two new vessels, port facilities and fare promotions on 24th May 2016, in a bold attempt to retain its Isle of Man business. Tynwald noted the offer but instructed the Department of Infrastructure to continue negotiations on the User Agreement, whilst considering all other options. The Company offer was withdrawn, making the future of services beyond 2026

although the Company was not consulted. However, the costs of replacing the Liverpool Landing Stage soared above £30 million, prompting the government to examine buying a site at the Princes Half Tide Dock to create its own terminal at a location 800 metres downstream from the Pier Head.

On 23rd May 2018 the Isle of Man government purchased the Company for £48.3 million, with an additional £76 million as a loan. The value of the *Ben-my-Chree* and *Manannan* was estimated at just £4.4 million by 2026. The deal assumed investment of £85 million in new or almost new vessels by 2023. Under

P&O's *Express* provides a contrast in fast craft design as she berths behind *Manannan*. *(Barry Edwards)*

unclear. Rumours circulated that the Isle of Man government was considering nationalising the Company, despite the medium-term fleet investment required. Meanwhile, Tynwald approved £80 million of harbour improvements, including to the King Edward Pier (£14.8 million) to berth a 'Heysham Max' vessel up to 142-metres, and a new linkspan on the Victoria Pier, capable of handling any vessel,

the new arrangements, the Company would operate at arm's length from the government from 1st January 2019. The Company was required to seek approval to enter into any agreement or contract worth more than £2.5 million, or before entering any mortgage for a ship.

The Isle of Man government launched a public consultation to understand more about service

The *Manannan* swings in Douglas harbour following her morning crossing from Belfast. *(Miles Cowsill)*

requirements, receiving 4,862 responses representing about 6% of the Island's population. Questions included preferred destinations, whether conventional ferries or fast craft should be used and whether ticket prices were considered fair. The results showed that 61% wanted the fast craft service to continue, while 33% preferred the year-round conventional ferry.

A new Sea Services Agreement was signed on 3rd June 2019 replacing the User Agreement, following approval in Tynwald. This specified replacement of *Ben-my-Chree* with a new vessel by the end of 2021. Tynwald approved the refinancing of the Company debt on 24th October 2019, supporting the recommendation for the Company to borrow the £76 million estimated cost from an outside source.

The Company launched their own on-line survey in November 2019 to gauge views on future investment in its new vessel. Questions sought views on items such as seating, catering, lounges, Wi-Fi coverage and charges.

Lars Ugland was appointed as a non-executive director of the Steam Packet Company and became Chairman at the beginning of April 2020, following the retirement of Robert Quayle on 31st March. Brian Thomson was later appointed to the role of Managing Director from 5th July 2021.

Planning permission was sought to move the Liverpool berth to the Princes Half Tide Dock. A ceremony at the site of the new Liverpool Terminal building on 17th January 2020 marked the start of work. The £38 million project was due for completion in July 2021, whilst plans were also announced to refurbish facilities at Heysham.

As the new decade began, life around the world

changed as the Covid-19 pandemic took hold. The Isle of Man required those arriving on the Island after 17th March 2020 to self-isolate for 14 days, but the borders were closed completely on 27th March. The *Ben-my-Chree* continued her twice-daily freight service to Heysham until *Manannan* took over the daytime sailings whilst *Arrow* made overnight trips to allow *Ben-my-Chree's* crew to have a full 14-day break and self-isolate in line with government guidelines. The *Ben-my-Chree* returned to operate overnight sailings

The Company was keen to ensure that the new vessel would continue long established tradition by taking an historic Steam Packet vessel name. A short list of four fondly remembered names was deemed fitting, comprising of *King Orry, Manx Maid, Manxman,* and *Mona's Isle*. The final decision was put to a public vote in November 2020 to ensure that everyone had the opportunity to participate in this important decision. More than 7,500 submitted their favourite name from the shortlist to inform the selection process.

Fleet mates. The **Ben-my-Chree** heads for Heysham as **Arrow** lays over in Douglas Bay. *(Barry Edwards)*

from 30th April, whilst *Manannan* covered daytime sailings.

After months of anticipation, the Company announced on 31st July 2020 that it had signed a contract with Hyundai Mipo Dockyard, Ulsan, South Korea for a new purpose-built ro-pax vessel. The new ship was to be slightly larger than *Ben-my-Chree,* with more passenger space and increased lane meterage for vehicles and designed to be more environmentally efficient with improved weather manoeuverability.

Manxman and *King Orry* emerged as the most popular choices by a considerable margin.

After much deliberation, it was revealed on Tuesday 1st December that the name of the vessel would be *Manxman,* thereby becoming the third ship in the Company's history to bear this name. *Manxman* embodies the Manx spirit, signifies national pride and is suitably enduring for a vessel that will take the Steam Packet into its bicentenary and beyond.

A new era was about to begin.

2

MANXMAN
HERITAGE

The Isle of Man Steam Packet Company has previously owned and operated two vessels named *Manxman*.

The first ship dated from 1904 and was built by Vickers, Sons and Maxim at Barrow in Furness to the order of the Midland Railway Company to operate excursions from its newly opened port at Heysham to the Isle of Man. On her trial run on 27th May, the crack steamer completed the 55-mile run in 2 hours 45 minutes. Her rail-connected services from all over northern England were instantly popular but ceased on the outbreak of the Great War in 1914, at which time *Manxman* was requisitioned by the Admiralty and converted into a seaplane carrier. At the end of hostilities, she was reconditioned back at Barrow, offered for sale and purchased by the Steam Packet in March 1920 before finally taking up the Liverpool service for her new owners on 14th July.

The *Manxman* joined a somewhat eclectic fleet of steamers, many which had come second hand to the Company. A dozen ships were involved in a multiplicity of cross-Irish Sea summer sailings bringing hordes of holiday makers from the industrial towns and smoky conurbations of Lancashire. Each town would have its own individual 'wakes week' when the factories and mills would close allowing workers to escape the industrial grime for the delights and clean air of the Isle Man. The ships were packed and at times there were so many arriving in Douglas that they berthed two or three deep along the Victoria Pier. In addition to sailings from English ports, significant traffic also emanated from the mining, ship building and steel making areas of Ayrshire, Glasgow, and the Scottish Lowlands while traffic from Ireland was also heavy, with regular sailings from both Belfast and Dublin. In sharp contrast, the winter period would see most of the fleet laid up when the lifeline service to Liverpool would require the operation of just two ships, each of which would operate a single daily crossing.

During the 1930s, the Steam Packet introduced four new steamers: the one and only centenary steamer *Lady of Mann* (1930), the impressive *Mona's Queen* (1934) and

The Midland Railway's **Manxman** (1904-1949) was acquired by the Steam Packet in 1920 and served for an impressive period of 45 years. *(John Clarkson)*

The second *Manxman* entered service in 1955 and was the final ship in a series of six similar post-war builds from Cammell Laird at Birkenhead. Originally a two-class steamer, her traditional interior typified the elegance of the period. *(all John Hendy)*

the sisters *Tynwald* and *Fenella* (1937). On the outbreak of World War Two, most of the fleet was once again requisitioned by the Admiralty and tragically the three newest vessels were lost, two of them, along with the old *King Orry* (1913), during the heroic evacuation of Dunkirk in May/June 1940.

At the war's end, like many others, the depleted fleet was mechanically in a bad way with much of the older tonnage somewhat the worse for wear after a punishing period during which essential maintenance was minimal. After a period trooping between Harwich and the Hook of Holland, *Manxman* was sold to breakers in Preston during 1949 after an exceptional career of 45 years in war and peace.

In order to rebuild the fleet, between 1946 and 1955

Cammell Laird at Birkenhead provided no fewer than six elegant steamers of a similar design largely based on the pre-war ships. The class was led by the new *King Orry* (1946), followed by *Mona's Queen* (1946), *Tynwald* (1947), *Snaefell* (1948), and *Mona's Isle* (1951). The final vessel in the series was named *Manxman* and was immediately recognisable from her half-sisters by having her lifeboats raised above Boat Deck level thereby giving passengers, good and all-round views of the sea. An improved and modern system of turbine engines also made her different from the rest of the class although this was not generally recognised by those who sailed in her.

The new *Manxman* was launched into the river Mersey on 8th February 1955 by Mrs J B Garside, wife of a Steam Packet Director, and later achieved a speed

The **Manxman** is seen in the shadow of the Liver Building whilst alongside the Landing Stage at Liverpool. *(John Clarkson)*

of 21.95 knots on the Skelmorlie measured mile in the Firth of Clyde. The ship cost £847,000 to build and completed her maiden voyage on 21st May 1955 replacing the veteran steamer *Viking* (1905) in the Manx fleet. With a gross tonnage of 2,495 she was licensed to carry as many as 2,393 passengers and crew. Her entry into service on 21st May (under the command of Captain P J Bridson) saw her cross to Liverpool with delegates of the Union of Post Office Workers returning from their annual conference.

The *Manxman's* somewhat masculine interior furnishings, although very traditional for the time, were

upmarket gentlemen's club. On the deck below, the darkly panelled and elegant dining saloon was carefully laid up with the traditional Steam Packet silver service, linen tablecloths, side plates, neatly folded napkins and carefully laid place settings which would quietly jangle as the ship's turbines drove her onwards towards her destination. On board *Manxman*, highly polished brass abounded, the bridge providing a particular pleasure with gleaming engine room telegraphs and binnacle beautifully set off by the beautifully maintained and varnished woodwork. Everything on board seemed to shout 'Quality!'

Winter service sees **Manxman** going astern past the Battery Pier at Douglas into the teeth of an easterly gale. *(Ferry Publications Library)*

Calmer times back in the River Mersey as **Manxman** prepares to sail for Douglas. *(Ferry Publications Library)*

really nothing out of the ordinary for 1955. However, as she grew older and her contemporaries were withdrawn from service one by one, her traditional features came to be enjoyed and appreciated by a completely new generation of travellers who saw in *Manxman*, the best that post-war British shipbuilding had provided. The former First Class, wooden-panelled, forward lounge on the Promenade Deck was stuffed full of deep and comfortable easy chairs and sofas and was complete with a fireplace and large mirror giving the impression of an

Throughout the 1950s, the country witnessed the rapid growth of private car ownership while in the following decade the construction of the first motorways made travel faster and the Isle of Man more accessible. The fleet of traditional Manx steamers were all built with wide and roomy promenades that were frequently used to carry a limited number of cars which, when the tide was right, could be driven directly on board from the quayside. Even double-decked buses were transhipped in this way to the island. In answer to the changing visitor demands, in 1962 the Steam Packet introduced its first car ferry *Manx Maid* followed by a near sister *Ben-my-Chree* in 1966. Their advent effectively saw the role of the remaining passenger-only steamers downgraded and for *Manxman*, long periods of winter lay-up awaiting the return of the tourists. In 1967, the Steam Packet abandoned its long established two class system and fares were adjusted accordingly between them. The decision was made following a general decline in passengers wishing to travel First Class and the increase in motorists crossing to the island. In order to meet the insatiable increase in car traffic, twin diesel-engined car ferries, *Mona's Queen* and *Lady of Mann* appeared in 1972 and 1976. With the withdrawal of the penultimate passenger steamer *Mona's Isle* in 1980, followers of coastal shipping became all too aware that

in *Manxman*, the Steam Packet were the owners of a once common but now unique type of vessel which had become the final traditional turbine passenger steamer in service anywhere in the British Isles. The sentiment was so strong that efforts to preserve the ship immediately swung into action.

Now under the command of Capt. Peter Corrin, *Manxman's* final season commenced in May 1982, and all too quickly ended with poignant farewells, the blowing of her whistle, flags flying, cheers, adieus and even tears at Ardrossan, then Fleetwood, Belfast, Dublin, Workington, and Llandudno. On the morning of 4th September, *Manxman* was back in the Mersey alongside the Landing Stage in readiness for a special 'Finished with Engines' charter when the whole river resounded to the echoes of her sonorous triple-chime steam whistle.

The **Manxman** under tow and showing the attractive sweep of her hull and her raised lifeboats which represented the most obvious difference from her half-sisters. *(John Clarkson)*

Leaving a damp Douglas later that afternoon for her return run, a brass band played, streamers were thrown, and an armada of local boats and yachts followed her out into the bay.

On 21st September it was announced that *Manxman* had been purchased by a sports and leisure company based in Preston and, with Capt. Corrin on the bridge for the final time, she sailed up the River Ribble to her new home on 3rd October. After 27 years, during which time she had been meticulously maintained, this intelligence initially seemed like good news but ultimately proved to be the opening chapter in a 30-year lingering fall from grace with *Manxman* surviving a partial sinking, arson, vandalism, and neglect on a grand scale. Ship preservation is, above all else, a very costly business and although eventually the Manxman

Steamship Company submitted ambitious plans for her future there was simply nowhere to moor the ship to ensure that she could be safe, and where restoration could commence.

Now painted all white, *Manxman* was moved from Preston to Liverpool in November 1990 thence to Hull in April 1994. Once there, she suffered the indignity of having a section cut out of her stem to fit her into the Ruscador Drydock. She opened for business as Britain's largest pub, but the venture soon failed, and the ship was targeted by vandals. A final move to Sunderland on the River Wear then took place where she was eventually broken up in the Pallion Shipyard during 2012.

It was a sad, but perhaps inevitable, end for a much-loved ship.

John Hendy

The **Manxman** is seen arriving at Preston in October 1982 at the start of her long period in static use. (*John Clarkson*)

Leaving Douglas on an afternoon return sailing to Belfast, *Manxman* sounds her magnificent triple-chime whistle. *(John Hendy)*

In November 1990, the *Manxman* was moved from Preston to the Trafalgar Dock in Liverpool prior to a further tow to Hull in 1994 where much of her original wood panelling was destroyed by fire. *(John Hendy)*

3

REMEMBERING MANXMAN

My first close sighting of *Manxman* came when I travelled on her from Liverpool to Douglas as a 12-year-old schoolboy in April 1961. She was then just half my age and the youngest, near sister, of her five post-war siblings. The *Manxman* was the newest vessel in the Isle of Man Steam Packet fleet and usually maintained the winter lifeline between Liverpool and Douglas, along with *King Orry* (IV). I remember sitting on the top of a lifejacket box on the Promenade (Boat) Deck, after she cleared the River Mersey, somewhat mesmerised by the enormity of my surroundings. Even then I knew I wanted to go to sea for a living, but I could not, in my wildest dreams, have imagined that in less than 20 years I would be one of her Masters.

Although I had been onboard her many times after joining the Company - then boasting a fleet of eight passenger and three cargo vessels - in May 1968, as AB in the Company's small cargo vessel *Ramsey*, and later as Second Officer in several Company vessels between 1969 and 1971, it wouldn't be until January 1971 that I would sail on the *Manxman* again. I well remember travelling by train from Barrow-in-Furness, where I had been on ship keeping and survey duty on the magnificent 1930-built *Lady of Mann* (I) in preparation for her last season in service, to join *Manxman* in Liverpool, then on winter service deputising for *Manx Maid* (II) and *Ben-my-Chree* (V) in overhaul, as Second Officer.

It was late afternoon as I approached the Princes Landing Stage and as she looked stately and majestic against the backdrop of the setting sun over New Brighton, it was easy to see just how *Manxman* and her sisters were often referred to as mini-Cunarders. Over the ensuing six years I would serve in her at various times as Second and Chief Officer, but by the end of 1977 the composition of the Company had altered quite significantly, with just two of the 'classic' steamers, *Mona's Isle* (V) and *Manxman*, remaining in the fleet.

The following year, almost ten years to the day since I joined the Company, I was immensely proud to be appointed to my first command, *Conister* (II), which in tandem with the converted *Peveril* (III) was operating a

Captain Peter Corrin. *(John Hendy)*

lift-on-lift-off container service between Liverpool and Douglas. Just over twelve months later I was thrilled to gain my first passenger vessel command, when I became Relief Master on *Mona's Isle* (V) taking her from Douglas to Belfast on 14th July. I remained as one of her Masters through the remainder of that summer and during a large period of her last year in service in 1980, which culminated in the poignant task of taking her on her final voyages, principally to and from Douglas, Liverpool, Llandudno, and Dublin, prior to laying her up in Morpeth Dock in Birkenhead on 28 August. But just a month prior to that, on 26th July 1980, I took command of *Manxman* for the first time, also on a sailing from Douglas to Belfast.

During the winter months of 1980/81 I found myself in command of *Conister* (II) or *Peveril* (III), before returning to the *Manxman* as one of her Masters for a large part of her penultimate season in 1981. The winter months, prior to re-joining *Manxman*, were spent as one of the regular masters of the roll-on-roll-off vessel *NF Jaguar* – later *Peveril* (IV) – which was chartered in 1981 to operate the new roll-on-roll-off (ro-ro) freight service between Douglas and Liverpool, replacing *Conister* (II) and *Peveril* (III). I have always felt enormously fortunate and proud to have been in command of all the Company vessels I was appointed to, but never more so than *Manxman* when, on a shared basis with my colleague the late Capt. David Hall, I was afforded the privilege of

Looking astern from **Manxman**'s flying bridge, her triple-chime whistle is shown to advantage. (*John Hendy*)

doing so during her final season. By then it was well known that, when she slipped her moorings from the Morpeth Dock, Birkenhead, on 25th May and steamed out into the River Mersey, it was almost certainly her last time in normal Steam Packet service.

Of course, I followed in the wake of some of the most respected and revered Masters who had served the Company with such distinction over several decades, including World War Two, and together with their officers and crews ensured *Manxman* remained in such fine condition after 27-years-service. I suspect most enthusiasts have a favourite ship, but in my experience, it is the crew who make the difference, and of all the Company vessels I had the pleasure of serving on and commanding, the pride in their ship exuded and displayed by the entire ship's complement of *Manxman* was apparent to all. However, the reason for her upcoming sale wasn't anything to do with her structural condition but simply that she had sadly outlived her commercial usefulness.

When the *Manxman* was built in 1955, there were still many passenger-only vessels plying major ferry routes, although car ferries were beginning to appear. By 1982, the *Manxman* was not only the last 'classic' turbine steamer in the Steam Packet fleet, but also anywhere in the British Isles. She had been well and truly superseded by car ferries and ro-ro vessels as commercial demands dictated. It is hard to believe now that she had a passenger certificate for 2,302 passengers and 60 crew and, even in her final season would, on many voyages, still carry well over 1,000 people, especially during the traditional 'wakes' holiday periods from Dublin, Belfast, Ardrossan and on day excursions from Fleetwood and Llandudno. There would often be many enthusiasts and devoted followers – of which she had many – onboard the excursions, soaking up the atmosphere as she silently and serenely glided through the water at an effortless 20 knots. Although built in the 1950s, her dimensions (length overall, 345-ft (105-m) beam 47-ft (14-m)) and design had its origins in the 1930s, so it was no surprise that in her later years she was in great demand from film

A view of **Manxman**'s busy fo'c'sle as she prepares to berth at the Victoria Pier at Douglas in July 1982. *(John Hendy)*

The **Manxman**'s gleaming brass bell as the ship lies alongside the pier at Llandudno. *(John Hendy)*

makers, not least, Barbra Streisand, who chartered her in September 1982 for part of her 1983 '*Yentl*' production. That, however, would be her last act as a Steam Packet vessel and the only task left for me was to deliver her safely from Liverpool to her new owners in Preston.

After I rang 'finished with engines' for the last time on 3rd October 1982, I did not expect to see her again or imagine that she would ever leave the Preston berth. I was incorrect on both counts. I visited her at the kind invitation of her original new owners and again, on three occasions, in her eventual final resting place in Sunderland, during the momentous efforts of those who valiantly gave of their time and talents to try and save her for posterity, right up until she was finally broken up in 2012. Visiting her was something of a surreal experience and it was akin to visiting an aged friend or relative for whom you knew the kindest action would be to let them peacefully slip away. And so it was that when the breaker's torches were extinguished and hammers fell silent, the life and soul of a very fine and special ship had finally come to an end.

So, I am sure you can understand how delighted I was to learn that the Company's new vessel was to be named *Manxman* in honour of her predecessors and my former command. Of course, her pre-war design meant that some of her facilities, machinery and equipment were outdated compared with today's standards, and even back in 1955 there was some suggestion that she should have been the Company's first car ferry. From a Master's perspective, one of the main differences between *Manxman* and today's vessels was certainly the lack of bow thrust propulsion, variable pitch propellers, bridge control and state-of-the-art navigational equipment. But none of that detracts from what a fine and much-loved Company servant she was and the ambassadorial manner, through her name, in which she carried not only hundreds of thousands of passengers but also the identity of the Isle of Man with her wherever she went. I am sure the new bearer of the name will do likewise with much distinction, and I am certain that all my successors who have the privilege of being in command of her, whether Manx or not, will feel immensely proud to have the responsibility of navigating her and the Company through the next and exciting chapter of its magnificent history.

Captain Peter Corrin

4 DESIGNED TO LAST

The 2019 Sea Services Agreement defined the criteria for the design of the Company's new vessel. It detailed that the commissioned vessel should be capable of: -

- operation using either marine fuel oil or liquified natural gas
- making the scheduled crossings in all seasons
- offering capacity for not less than 800 passengers
- including capacity for 1,250 lane metres of freight capacity, with freight high space (over 4.8-metres) at least 10% more than that offered on the *Ben-my-Chree*
- taking into account the outcome of the Isle of Man Government's 2018 Public Survey
- paying due regard to the Government's policy to reduce emissions

- complying with the 2020 International Maritime Organisation's Sulphur Limit Regulations

Service introduction for the new vessel was given a back-stop date of 31st December 2022; this was later amended to 31st December 2023 to reflect the travel and work constraints imposed following the coronavirus pandemic.

The Steam Packet had a long association with marine design consultancy Hart Fenton dating back over two decades to when the two companies were under the common ownership of Sea Containers. The relationship continued after Hart Fenton was taken over by Houlder in 2006. The team supported the design, specification, and build process of *Ben-my-Chree* and subsequently assisted with the structural design and stability calculations for the installation of the vessel's extension,

The **Ben-my-Chree** swings in the harbour as she arrives in Douglas with a well-laden sailing during her maiden 1998 season. Back-up vessel **King Orry** is berthed on the Victoria Pier. *(Miles Cowsill)*

A striking aerial view of a lightly loaded **Ben-my-Chree** after the new accommodation block was added to her superstructure in 2004. She is sporting the new ship livery applied after 2008. *(Ferry Publications Library)*

to house the on-board bar and Niarbyl reserved lounge. In 2008, Houlder was awarded the contract for the conversion of the fastcraft *Manannan*, transforming her from a military vessel to a high-speed passenger ferry in a £20 million project. Houlder provided a wide range of technical, design and drafting support during the work, which almost doubled her passenger capacity and was then the largest conversion of a high-speed catamaran ever undertaken. Houlder later designed the removable

mezzanine deck for *Manannan*, increasing her capacity for motorcycles during peak-season race events by 10%.

The prospect of a new vessel for the Isle of Man had been considered by Houlder for some time and, as the negotiations on the Sea Services Agreement headed to a conclusion, the company produced preliminary sketches of an outline design. The workstream progressed to the production of a formal proposal to support development of the concept design, which in turn led to the compilation of detailed tender specification for shipyards, including general arrangement drawings.

David Wing, Director, Ship Design & Engineering, at Houlder, led the team from the start of the relationship. As well as assisting with the concept specification and general arrangement for *Manxman* in the early stages, he visited the shortlisted shipyards with the Steam Packet team and offered specialist knowledge to help evaluate their suitability. Houlder continued to support the project throughout the stages of plan approval, during contract and technical discussions, and with specialist naval architecture advice. The close working relationship ensured that the design of *Manxman* flawlessly reflected the Company's requirements, optimised by Houlder's operational experience and comprehensive understanding of the challenges of operating passenger vessels in the Irish Sea.

Mike Simpson was also involved from inception and inputted substantially to the initial design, general arrangement, and specification, fully utilising his over-40-years' experience to understand the key project drivers and ensure they were fully recognised in the design. Meanwhile, Rob Lee was responsible for coordinating the plan approval correspondence throughout the design and build stage, collating input from across the Steam Packet, Houlder and SeaQuest teams to deliver a coherent set of review comments.

The Sea Services Agreement was compiled without a specific vessel in mind but used *Ben-my-Chree* as a benchmark comparator. The specification for enhanced capacity was challenging, given the size constraints imposed on the vessel by the harbour facilities in Douglas, Heysham and Liverpool. Furthermore, safety regulations had changed significantly over the quarter century since *Ben-my-Chree* was built. So, the design requirements for the new vessel were very different from

The **Ben-my-Chree** undergoing one of her annual refits at Birkenhead. *(Steam Packet)*

her predecessor. The Company was also keen to ensure that customer preferences were incorporated wherever possible, and the Houlder team was able to fine-tune the emerging design to include key elements following publication of the results of the public survey in April 2020. Multiple workstreams ran in parallel during this phase to ensure that deadlines would be met.

The project presented two design challenges. Firstly,

What might have been - a ro-pax design proposal by Cammell Laird shipbuilders. *(Cammell Laird)*

DESIGNED TO LAST

Houlder undertook several projects on **Manannan**, including her original conversion from a military vessel and the addition of a removable mezzanine deck. *(Miles Cowsill)*

to provide a dependable lifeline service throughout the harsh winter weather conditions on the lifeline route between Douglas and Heysham. And secondly, to increase passenger capacity, especially during the peaks of traffic at annual events such as the TT Races.

The requirement for 1,200 lane-metres of freight capacity, coupled with the need to offer wider lane widths to accommodate the increase in vehicle sizes since *Ben-my-Chree* was introduced, placed pressure on the vessel's lightweight capacity. With freight vehicles becoming taller as well as wider, increasing capacity for these vehicles was not as simple as raising deck height; higher deck heights affect the vessels' stability, increase lightweight, and require longer ramps to access the

The development of several iterations of the design allowed different elements to be tested to ensure optimisation of the final product. Note the different funnel design and window configuration from the as-built vessel. *(Houlder)*

upper deck, all of which had to be fitted within the vessel length constraints imposed by the ports of operation.

One major design challenge was to overcome the operational problems that precluded passenger cars being loaded early on *Ben-my-Chree* for the nightly 02:15 sailing from Heysham to Douglas. The new vessel design permits cars to be loaded earlier into a dedicated area on the upper deck, ahead of freight traffic, thereby allowing passengers to make the most of onboard facilities and cabin occupancy during their crossing.

These operational issues were exacerbated by the need to incorporate equipment redundancy driven by the modern requirement for new vessels to have 'Safe Return to Port' capability. This requires modern passenger ships to be designed to ensure that essential systems remain operational after a fire or flood, with the ship able to proceed to a safe port under its own power. Persons onboard must be accommodated in a 'safe area' during the return to port, with basic services such as food, water, sanitation, medical care, lighting, and ventilation, maintained for all. In more challenging circumstances, regulations require some essential systems to remain operational for three hours to support an orderly evacuation of the vessel. This poses a significant test to the ship's designers.

The *Manxman's* design incorporates food serveries forward and aft on the vessel so that each space is

Houlder produced a number of computer generated concept designs for **Manxman**, that gradually evolved into the finished product. *(Houlder)*

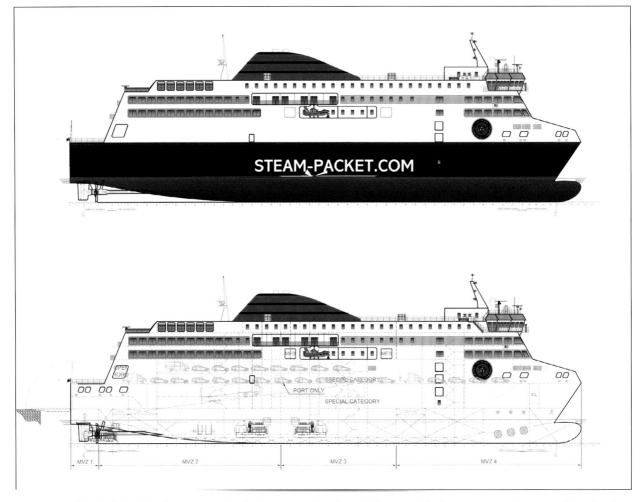

Some 300 detailed design plans were needed for the construction phase of **Manxman**. This view shows an early concept illustrating the internal ramp used to access the upper car decks. *(Houlder)*

capable of supplying passenger and crew sustenance in the event of the other being incapacitated. Considerable thought went into the evacuation plan to ensure that the design could meet the Company's requirement to use Marine Evacuation Systems rather than lifeboats.

The *Manxman* was designed to balance efficiency and stability, so her hull form is sculpted to ensure a smooth motion on the water, and the bulbous bow reduces the energy needed to power the vessel, thereby improving fuel consumption. At the stern, her twin rudders and propellers are designed to reduce vibration, increase efficiency, and provide additional manoeuverability. Three powerful bow thrusters, offering twice the output of *Ben-my-Chree*, give *Manxman* additional versatility

MANXMAN: Design features

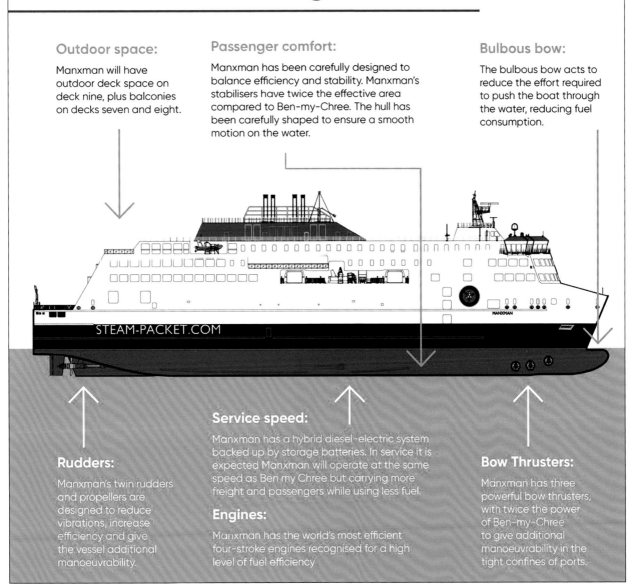

Outdoor space:

Manxman will have outdoor deck space on deck nine, plus balconies on decks seven and eight.

Passenger comfort:

Manxman has been carefully designed to balance efficiency and stability. Manxman's stabilisers have twice the effective area compared to Ben-my-Chree. The hull has been carefully shaped to ensure a smooth motion on the water.

Bulbous bow:

The bulbous bow acts to reduce the effort required to push the boat through the water, reducing fuel consumption.

STEAM-PACKET.COM

MANXMAN

Rudders:

Manxman's twin rudders and propellers are designed to reduce vibrations, increase efficiency and give the vessel additional manoeuvrability.

Service speed:

Manxman has a hybrid diesel-electric system backed up by storage batteries. In service it is expected Manxman will operate at the same speed as Ben my Chree but carrying more freight and passengers while using less fuel.

Engines:

Manxman has the world's most efficient four-stroke engines recognised for a high level of fuel efficiency

Bow Thrusters:

Manxman has three powerful bow thrusters, with twice the power of Ben-my-Chree to give additional manoeuvrability in the tight confines of ports.

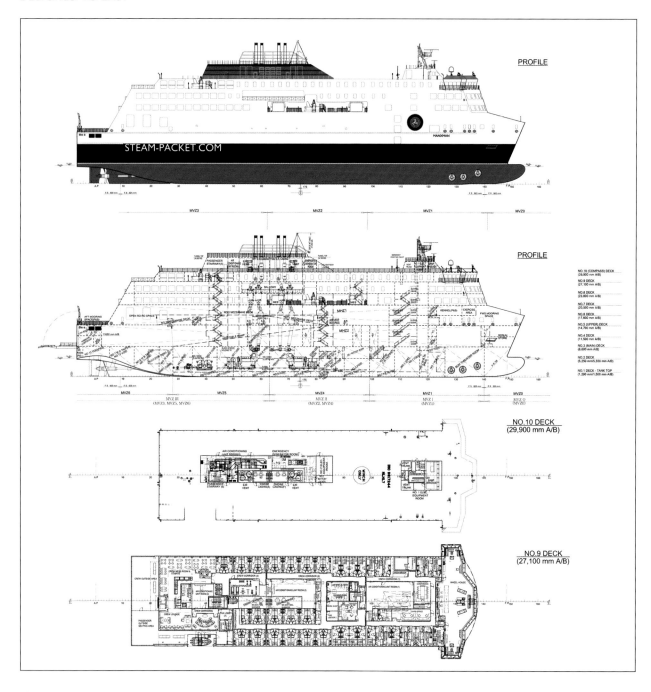

PROFILE

PROFILE

NO.10 (COMPASS) DECK
(29,900 mm A/B)
NO.9 DECK
(27,100 mm A/B)
NO.8 DECK
(23,800 mm A/B)
NO.7 DECK
(20,500 mm A/B)
NO.6 DECK
(17,800 mm A/B)
NO.5 (UPPER) DECK
(14,760 mm A/B)
NO.4 DECK
(11,500 mm A/B)
NO.3 (MAIN) DECK
(8,600 mm A/B)
NO.2 DECK
(5,250 mm/5,550 mm A/B)
NO.1 DECK - TANK TOP
(1,290 mm/1,500 mm A/B)

NO.10 DECK
(29,900 mm A/B)

NO.9 DECK
(27,100 mm A/B)

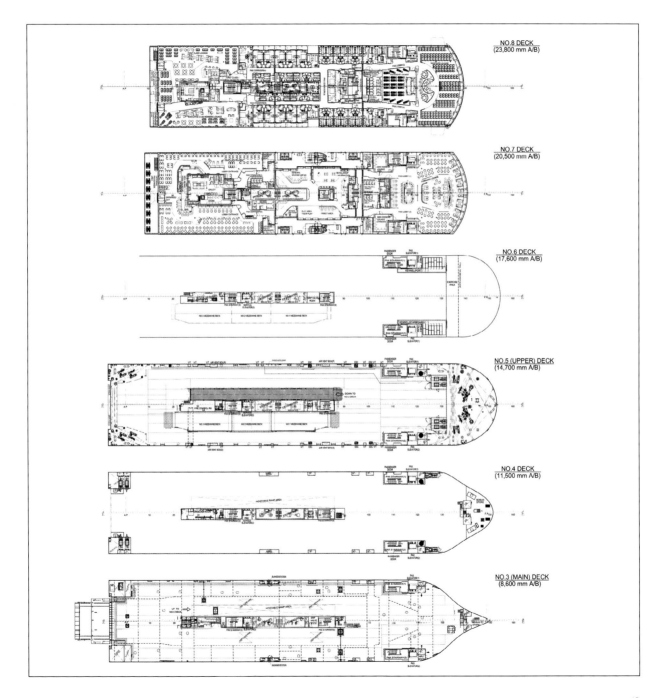

NO.8 DECK
(23,800 mm A/B)

NO.7 DECK
(20,500 mm A/B)

NO.6 DECK
(17,600 mm A/B)

NO.5 (UPPER) DECK
(14,700 mm A/B)

NO.4 DECK
(11,500 mm A/B)

NO.3 (MAIN) DECK
(8,600 mm A/B)

Congratulations to the Isle of Man Steam Packet Company

Wärtsilä is proud to have supplied a fully integrated hybrid propulsion and navigation system on the Manxman. The integrated system optimises operations and allows flexibility for future fuels as IOMSPC drives to decarbonise operations.

Read more at wartsila.com/marine

during port movements.

Design became an iterative process, as creative solutions were sought to reduce the vessel's lightweight. One example of this was the innovative interaction between the freight deck and mooring spaces on Deck 5. Elsewhere, the shipyard looked at the proposed arrangement of watertight compartments below the main deck in the initial design, and devised a practical solution to reduce their number as they added their construction perspective to the project. The desire for diesel electric propulsion gave plenty of flexibility from the outset. The future trajectory of green fuel technology was unclear during the early stages of the design process, although methanol is now increasingly the fuel of choice. Options for a Liquified Natural Gas (LNG) solution were evaluated in the design phase;

supply was identified as an issue, and LNG requires a significant allocation of storage space on board, bringing its own lightweight issues to the design, and impacting on the vessel's freight carrying capacity. The final choice of engines was driven partly by their potential adaptability to future fuel options, but also by fuel consumption. The Wärtsilä solution was selected from the green perspective, but also from its ability to operate from the ship's electricity in port, allowing engines to be shut down, thereby eliminating idling and harmful emissions.

The *Manxman* is powered by the Guinness World Records 'world's most efficient four-stroke diesel engine', with two eight-cylinder and two ten-cylinder engines, which are recognised for high levels of fuel efficiency and reduced exhaust emissions. Steam Packet Fleet

Wightlink's 2018-built *Victoria of Wight* bears many external similarities to *Manxman*. *(John Hendy)*

Operations Manager Jim Royston noted that the Wärtsilä engines were selected for several reasons. "The firm not only had the experience and track-record required for the project, but the engine's diesel consumption is on average around eight-per-cent lower than similar sized engines available on the market. In terms of system integration and operational optimisation, we will be able to run a variety of engine combinations to ensure they are always running as close to their most efficient, while suiting both *Manxman* and the routes it will serve." The *Manxman* is planned to operate at the same speed as *Ben-my-Chree* whilst consuming considerably less fuel to carry more freight traffic and passengers.

The Wärtsilä scope included the fitting of Wärtsilä 31 engines, electrical and automation systems, the energy storage system, and propulsion machinery, including transverse thrusters. Wärtsilä also supplied their latest NACOS Platinum integrated navigation system along with a newly developed, ground-breaking Bridge Console Design. This provides a single common software platform for all navigation applications including Dynamic Positioning. A Low Loss Concept power distribution system delivers higher efficiency, lower weight and volume, and a high system

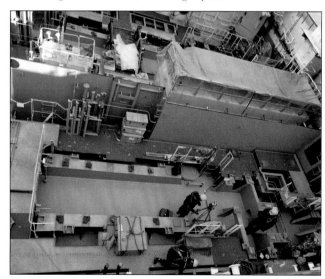

An unusual view of the engine compartment of *Manxman* prior to completion. *(Steam Packet)*

A view of one the early stages of the construction of **Manxman** as equipment is craned into place. *(Steam Packet)*

redundancy, reducing and eliminating the need for supply (pulse) transformers to the frequency converters, especially those supplying electric propulsion. Wärtsilä transverse thrusters combine high thrust values with compact dimensions to support mooring and harbour operations. The Wärtsilä solution included fitting of an Aquarius® Ballast Water Treatment Systems to help prevent invasive species devastating the marine environment. The *Manxman* will meet global ballast water discharge regulatory obligations through a filter UV system that meets IMO, UGA and USCG (type) approvals.

Design of the passenger areas was left to the SMC Design team. Houlder worked to incorporate their requirements with an interactive feedback process to ensure that evacuation and fire safety requirements were fully incorporated at each stage. There was a clear requirement from the passenger survey for a wide variety of cabins for a vessel of this size, but the outline design allocated space and a weight allowance for them, with their detailed design left for SMC. However, it was important that cabin accommodation was located away from areas of the ship that might be susceptible to noise and/or vibration to meet cruise ship standards of comfort; this required the shipyard to undertake a significant amount of work to model noise measurements. One key difference from *Ben-my-Chree* was to ensure that crew facilities were of sufficient quality and scope to permit them to live on board the vessel for up to a fortnight at a time.

The Houlder team's previous experience delivering Wightlink's new vessel *Victoria of Wight* in 2018, which has a similar external profile, enabled learning to be transferred to the new vessel.

Adapting the design to fit the proposed ports of operation was challenging in a time of pandemic travel restrictions, with the new terminal in Liverpool still at the construction stage. The latter was designed to

accommodate *Manannan's* passenger gangway entrance, so *Manxman* was designed with a passenger door in the same position. Houlder undertook a separate mooring study for the Steam Packet to help specify the shore changes needed in Douglas to accommodate *Manxman* on the linkspan and allow her to berth safely and securely in all weathers.

When *Ben-my-Chree* was built by Van der Giessen de Noord, she was designed primarily as a freight vessel, with passenger accommodation added, so her construction was driven by efficiency. Her stabilisers are sufficient to meet operational requirements but are not to modern cruise ship standards, so *Manxman* presented an opportunity for significant improvement, albeit within the constraints of lightweight. A vessel of this size and length is sensitive to wave periods, so seakeeping studies were commissioned to better understand predicted speed loss and power requirements to maintain a reliable service. The resulting installation of intelligent stabilisers, which combine twice the surface area of

Further views of the engine compartments, with the Wärtsilä engines being craned aboard whilst still in their transit protection wrapping. *(Steam Packet)*

those on *Ben-my-Chree*, with the ability to 'read' wave patterns and pro-actively address emerging weather conditions whilst reducing unnecessary 'drag', significantly enhancing passenger comfort.

In the early stages of the project the focus was very much business-led, to ensure that the design incorporated customer requirements and the commercial needs of the Company. As design progressed, so the emphasis switched to optimising the maintenance and accessibility capabilities of the finished vessel. The iterative process made sure that the shipyard's objective of simplifying the construction process was balanced against the future need to maintain the ship in service. The role of Houlder moved on to offer help, advice, and guidance as an efficient design emerged.

As Jim Royston noted, "Throughout this project, Houlder has effectively integrated with the Company team, which has been hugely beneficial to this build. We last worked with Houlder on a newbuild back in the early 1990s, and a lot has changed since then in terms of regulations and design standards. Through an in-depth understanding of our operations, Houlder has provided frictionless mediation between ourselves and HMD, offering constructive perspectives on challenges faced, and working proactively to minimise delays relating to class society approval. Essentially, it's a service we didn't know we needed, but one we're incredibly grateful to now have access to."

CHAPTER FIVE

A CUSTOMER-DRIVEN REVOLUTION

With *Manxman's*, size, shape, and broad configuration determined by Houlder's design work, attention turned to the internal fit-out of the vessel. The 2019 Sea Services Agreement again provided guidance, detailing that the commissioned vessel should be capable of passenger facilities to a quality comparable with that provided by leading Irish Sea and English Channel ferry companies, including the quality and variety of food and beverages, furnishing and decoration, customer service offered by staff, and cleaning and maintenance of all areas.

The Company commissioned Island Global Research to undertake research to understand more about the on-board facilities prioritised by customers for the new vessel. An on-line survey in late 2019 produced a helpful 8,470 responses, split between 5,173 Manx residents (61%) and 3,297 off-island customers (39%). Respondents prioritised their five most important facilities from a list of 13 provided in the survey, creating the following overall ranking: -

1. More tables in the standard seating areas, Niarbyl lounge and/or Pet Lounge
2. Introduction of a quiet lounge/quieter areas
3. A dedicated cafe area to eat and drink away from other seating areas.
4. Increased availability of standard cabins
5. More places to buy hot drinks, snacks, and cold food near your seat.

The three most important services to be included on the new vessel were seen to be: -

1. A wider choice of food and drink
2. More charging/plug points
3. Improved toilet facilities

Specific interest groups also prioritised the availability of a Cinema Lounge and a Children's Play Area, an increase in the availability of Pet Lounges and pet-friendly cabins, and better accessibility (notably the provision of larger lifts from the vehicle deck, identified as a particular priority for those using wheelchair-accessible cabins).

From the outset, the Board was keen to ensure that the innovative design of *Manxman* was matched by a step-change in quality of on-board experience to surpass the requirements of the Sea Services Agreement. The new flagship vessel presented a once in a generation opportunity to transform perceptions of both the Island and the Company, so the choice of interior designer was critical to the future success of the project. The design partner needed relevant experience in the ferry market, with a proven track record of delivering vessels to match those high ambitions.

London-based SMC Design was founded in 1988, initially as an interior design business, growing to become a graphic design and artwork consultancy a decade later. The company pioneered maritime interior design by successfully delivering many large-scale projects and building an international portfolio of clients. SMC Design is now an interdisciplinary design consultancy embracing interior and architectural design, branding and art consultancy working in the marine, hospitality, leisure, and retail industries. Prominent across the shipping sector, the consultancy has delivered major projects for Cunard, Saga Cruises, DFDS and P&O Ferries. Of particular interest to the Steam Packet was the fact that SMC had worked with Houlder on previous projects and were familiar with producing work for island communities in their interior design of *Victoria of Wight* for Wightlink.

SMC Design were appointed in August 2021 after a

competitive tender process. General arrangement drawings had already been produced by Houlder, with many items such as lifts and stairwells hard wired into the design, but SMC had the ability to adjust, for example, the galley and interior space layout to optimise passenger flows around the vessel. However, there was a relatively short period to complete the work before the plans passed to the shipyard for the construction phase. SMC were experienced designers of all scales of ship and treated the *Manxman* design process identically to

Roberts, with Senior Art Consultant Emmie Ratter providing specialist support on the selection of on-board artwork. They quickly built strong relationships with the other partners delivering *Manxman*, particularly Jim Royston and the Steam Packet personnel. The Company team distinguished themselves by taking bold and innovative decisions from the outset, often taking the harder, correct decision, rather than the easiest option. The combination of passionate designers and an engaged client made sparks fly. The atmosphere at

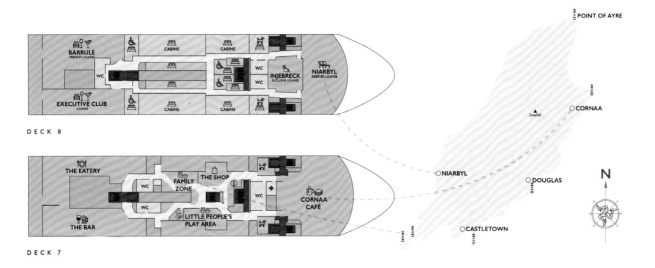

Facilities on *Manxman* have been named after 'touch points' around the Isle of Man to bring an air of familiarity to the vessel. *(SMC Design)*

previous cruise and ferry commissions to create the best possible design. The iterative process required attention to detail, so for example, shower door designs took 3½ weeks of intense work to produce something that worked effectively.

The team was led by Senior Associate Liam Kirk, supported by Senior Designer/Project Manager FF&E Liz Richardson, Associates Matthew Fyvie, and Alun

the shipyard became that of a large family working together to achieve a seamless, common goal.

The SMC team undertook considerable research to understand the characteristics of the Island and its people before commencing the project design. The process was helped by having a Shetlander, Emmie Ratter, on the team, and Liverpudlian Alun Roberts who was familiar with the Island. The SMC objective

Preliminary sketches for the Cornaa Café Lounge, forward on Deck 7 of *Manxman*, portray the light and airy impression of the 'living room' of the vessel. *(SMC Design)*

The design sketch for The Eatery, aft on Deck 7 of *Manxman*. *(SMC Design)*

The Niarbyl Lounge, forward on Deck 8 of *Manxman*, gives passengers stunning views across the bow of the vessel. *(SMC Design)*

was to produce a holistic design that encapsulated elements of the culture, heritage, and landscape of the Isle of Man, making Islanders feel at home whilst on board, yet inspiring visitors to experience the Manx environment from the moment they step aboard *Manxman*. The internal design was all about the Island.

The coronavirus pandemic brought its own

the character of the island community. These montages became touch points to which the team referred to as the design unfolded to ensure that the sense of familiarity was inherent throughout *Manxman*. Core space designs were inspired by the natural habitats of the Island, using colour, texture, and pattern to reflect contrasting landscapes, whilst bringing out a sense of

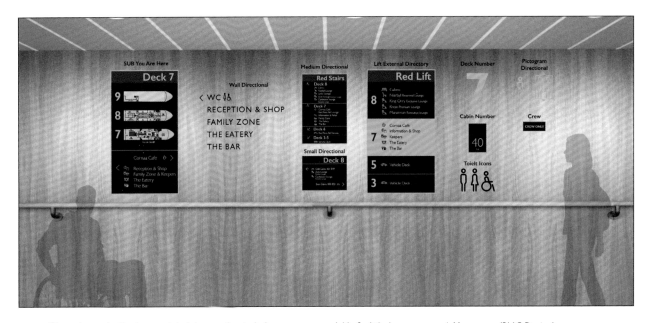

Clear signage in the house style is imperative to help passengers quickly find their way around *Manxman*. (SMC Design)

challenges when travel restrictions were imposed; this prompted creative approaches to working arrangements between the teams. Iterations to the design were pitched and approved through video calls, with fabric and colour samples being held up to computer screens for review.

SMC produced montages of imagery to draw inspiration of the elements that exemplify the character of the Isle of Man - a mixture of nature, produce, tourist attractions, wildlife, the mystical heritage, and

rugged scenery, heritage, natural environment, colour hues and the sheer enchantment of the Isle of Man. Wood finishes were employed to bring out the natural rawness of the island; oak reflects heritage and strength, dark wood picks up the dark skies in bold colours, lighter finishes provide contrast and warmth. Texture was added through the design of carpets. Everything placed on board related directly to other features, not just because it looked nice. All this needed to be encapsulated into a timeless, classic design, so that

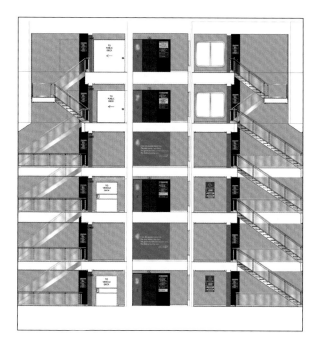

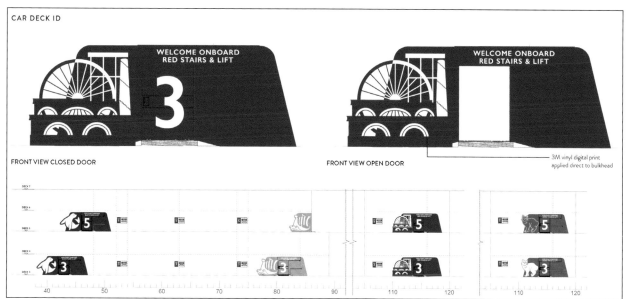

The use of vivid colour throughout the stairwells, with bold images of Island icons, helps orientate passengers from the moment they board *Manxman*. (*SMC Design*)

Manxman remains contemporary and relevant for the duration of her service with the Company.

SMC's in-house art consultancy enabled artwork to be integrated into the design from the beginning, through commissioning pieces that celebrated the skills of Manx-based artists, within the context of the *Manxman* palette. Liam Kirk and Emmie Ratter visited local art exhibitions with Brian Thomson and Jim

would be exhibited to an ever-changing audience.

Cruise ships and hotels work best when they have a meticulously designed flow and uniformity throughout their design. These principles have been imported into *Manxman*. So, the style of each passenger space varies to provide personality to the ship, but each is aligned with its neighbour so that the journey around the ship feels a holistic experience.

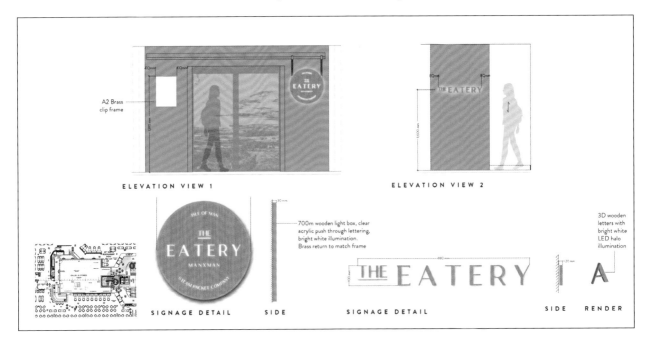

Lounge signage is carefully designed to integrate holistically into the overall look and feel of each venue on **Manxman**. *(SMC Design)*

Royston to meet artists and commission works appropriate for each area of the vessel. Careful selection ensured that the resultant tight, concise brand bonded every facet of the design into a rounded experience, so nothing feels out of place. The enthusiasm of the Island-based artists provided inspiration to the team, and they appreciated the opportunity of the international platform on which their commissions

The interior design reflects compass points to create 'a familiar vessel reflecting an Island of contrasts, rich with the spoils of nature, honest materials and a warm welcome'. Lounges on *Manxman* have been given local names – the Cornaa Café, the Niarbyl Reserved Lounge, the Injebreck exclusive Lounge, and the Barrule Premium Lounge. There are little ticks of the corporate red hue throughout the vessel that binds the design together.

The Manx experience was deemed to start the moment passengers board *Manxman*, whilst providing orientation around the ship's design. There are big bold exit points from each car deck, with the first icon representing the start of the story. The red stairwell incorporates images of the Laxey Wheel, the green stairwell a Manx cat, the yellow stairwell a Viking with hints of the Celtic past, traditional produce such as kippers and a nod to the fairies. The red reflects landmarks, from the Laxey wheel to the Tower of Refuge in Douglas Bay and the lighthouses dotted around the Island. Green represents the wildlife and natural beauty, featuring the Manx cat, the Northern Lights, and the night skies, with suitable acknowledgement of the Island's vegetation.

ELEVATION VIEW 1

SIGNAGE DETAIL

SIDE

RENDER

Frosting to back panel to prevent text from being read backwards from behind

3D wooden letters surface mounted to glass panel

longship, and the blue stairwell a seal. These icons are designed to be memorable to children, even if adults sometimes forget.

The journey to the passenger decks starts with these icons, and is punctuated throughout by collages, presented in the blue stairwell as features of the crossing, including birds, sea life, ships, and the coastlines of Ireland, Scotland, England, and the Isle of Man. The yellow stairway portrays the Island's heritage,

Although *Manxman* is small by cruise standards, it is important that passengers understand the layout quickly to make the most of their time on board. So, wayfinding is strong, with a good legible contrast through black and gold colours providing continuity with the brand. The SMC team worked closely with the Sight Matters to understand how the needs of the visually impaired could be accommodated. So, matte finishes are used to reduce glare, with wayfinding presented at eye level in

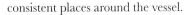

consistent places around the vessel.

All *Manxman's* main passenger facilities are found on deck 7, with a variety of supplementary accommodation options available on deck 8.

DECK 7

Deck 7 is cleverly designed so that passengers can walk a 'figure of eight' route around the deck to stretch their legs during a crossing. Most car passengers will access *Manxman's* passenger facilities via the red (port) and green (starboard) stairways and lifts, which bring them into the bright and welcoming Forward Lounge.

The Forward Lounge takes advantage of full height panoramic windows to provide a bright and airy space for 198 passengers, with a variety of seating types. The Cornaa Café offers a range of hot drinks and light snacks in this relaxed and informal setting, which will become a popular meeting point for families taking advantage of the banquette seating – the 'living room' of the vessel. Other decks can be accessed by two passenger lifts and stairways. The Lounge takes its palette from the villages and urban areas of the Island, reflecting the old Manx stone of Peel and Castletown and the colours of typical tiled finishes. Roof lichen is subtly reflected in the carpet design, whilst hexagon shapes pay tribute to the Island's characteristic lighthouses.

Two Paws Pet Lounges - each seating 12 passengers and providing outstanding facilities for their pets – are coloured to match the adjacent red and green stairways and lifts. These Pet Lounges were ranked high in importance amongst the Island community, and the process of their design went through multiple iterations to consider the interests of a wide variety of pets. The result is a pair of stunning lounges, complete with a dedicated walking area for pets, a first for the ferry

industry. A First Aid/Adult changing room and toilet facilities are also provided in this Lounge.

Strong visual wayfinding and signage guides passengers towards the midships facilities of *Manxman*, with a natural flow on both port and starboard sides to reach the central Family Zone, the Retail Shop, and the Information Desk. The Family Zone is the heart of the ship, a focal point for families with young children. The soft play area for 'little people' is bespoke designed by Tiger Player, one of the leading specialist designers in the industry and this will bring families together in this central area. The adjacent Parent & Child room was one of the first elements that the Steam Packet team wanted to introduce onto the vessel.

The branding of the Little People's Play Area extends to a range of merchandise in the shop. The shop area is much enlarged from *Ben-my-Chree*, allowing a full range of quality merchandise to be displayed alongside locally sourced products, showcasing the best of the Island on clear, open shelving. The shop's palette reflects the artisan and retail nature of the space, with neutral, earthy tones giving a feeling of familiarity.

The perimeter walls of the Family Zone incorporate a timeline showing the build and delivery of *Manxman*.

The aft Bar and the Eatery restaurant occupy the remainder of the space on Deck 7; these are linked but divided at the same time. The self-service restaurant lies on the port side with the bar to starboard, both wrapped around a central galley equipped with state-of-the-art cooking facilities. The space is designed to be walked around as part of the natural 'figure of eight' flow and gives access to an external seating area that offers stunning views across the stern of the ship. Outside seating is of cruise ship standard with carefully designed high quality balustrades at the cutting edge of current ferry design.

The aft Bar creates the feeling of a country pub with a variety of comfortable seating areas, making strong use of natural light. *(SMC Design)*

The moorlands and heathlands of the Isle of Man provide a welcoming theme in the Executive Club Lounge. *(SMC Design)*

The Barrule Premium Lounge uses a woodland palette to create an atmosphere of warm sophistication. *(SMC Design)*

The inside area is very open, with a selection of glazing visuals giving hints of accent colours. The palette is based on the agricultural aspects of the Island, bringing to life the colours of the stone of Manx cottages and walls, a ploughed or harvested field, with little nods to agricultural fitments. So light fittings comprise of the kind of little metal pieces that might be found in agricultural outbuildings. The Company was keen to showcase their new locally sourced menus to emphasise modern 'field to fork' provenance, and this is

provided throughout Decks 7 and 8. Public showers are provided for all passengers on Deck 8.

DECK 8

The passenger facilities on Deck 8 bring several new concepts to Manx travel.

At the forward end of *Manxman* lies the Niarbyl Reserved seating Lounge with 283 seats specially positioned to take advantage of wide panoramic views across the bow. This replicates facilities on *Ben-my-Chree*,

Each lounge is distinguished by unique typefaces and branding to give an exclusive feel. *(Miles Cowsill)*

complemented by the fresh feel of this environment. The Bar feels more like a country pub, with extremely comfortable, larger seats, including traditional leather banquettes, and warmer timbers to enhance the welcoming feel. The logotype and colouring are consistent across both restaurant and bar, giving a commonality to the space.

The quality of toilet facilities is one of the most important ways in which the customer focus of a vessel can be judged, and the specification on *Manxman* is to the highest standards. The same quality of facilities is

but SMC were keen to differentiate this area to create a fresh, relaxing, and engaging space. The palette is based on the coastal areas of the Isle of Man, with the strata of cliffs and the warm purples and pinks of coastal flowers, complemented by a carpet incorporating the accents of rock pools and dappled waters. Lighting is based on lighthouse bulbs, with a feature ceiling pendant.

The process of choosing the seating was protracted to ensure that the size, depth, and width would optimise passenger comfort. And there are areas of banquette

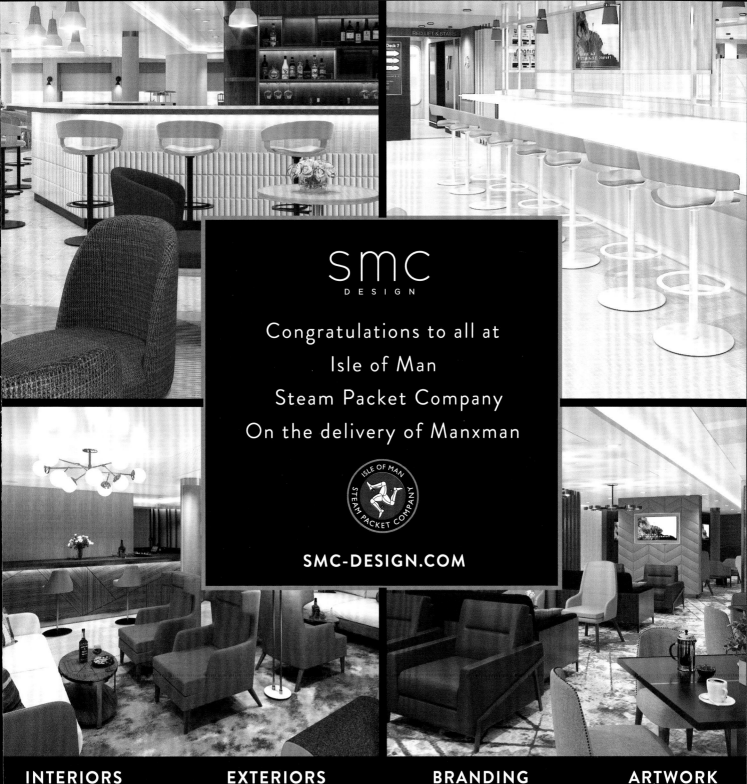

SMC
D E S I G N

Congratulations to all at
Isle of Man
Steam Packet Company
On the delivery of Manxman

SMC-DESIGN.COM

INTERIORS   **EXTERIORS**   **BRANDING**   **ARTWORK**

The Café Lounge takes advantage of full size picture windows to provide a bright and welcoming seating area on **Manxman**. (Miles Cowsill)

The Barrule Premium Lounge offers passengers a variety of seating options with outstanding sea views. (Miles Cowsill)

The Eatery reflects the colours of the agricultural scene on the Isle of Man. (Miles Cowsill)

CORNAA CAFÉ
WC
THE SHOP
INFORMATION DESK
THE FAMILY ZONE
THE EATERY
THE BAR
Deck 7

The passageway on Deck 8 at the entrance to the Barrule Lounge (*Miles Cowsill*)

One of the stairwell illustrations designed by the graphic design team at SMC. (*Miles Cowsill*)

seating for those who wish to meet up. The branding of this area pays homage to the Celtic traditions of the Island and the Manx language, with a modern elegant twist on ancient writings balancing the historic and modern cultures of the Isle of Man.

Midships, in the centre of *Manxman*, lies the exclusive Injebreck Lounge with 26 airline-style flat bed seats. The entrance portal evokes the dark skies that are a feature of the Island, with stars and moons to introduce the idea of relaxation and a quiet environment. Injebreck is represented by a contour map that pinpoints the location. Inside, the ceiling sports a simple star design, whilst the carpet is subtly based on the surface of the moon, transporting passengers to a

very different onboard experience. The seats incorporate a flash of red, to reflect Steam Packet branding and add a little warmth. Passengers will have access to a pantry, with a selection of drinks and pastries. Access to the Injebreck Lounge is by key card, giving the space an air of exclusivity.

A key feature of *Manxman* is the variety of cabins on offer; these lie midships on Deck 8 and are carefully positioned to minimise disturbance from ship noise and vibration. The *Manxman* sports 10 double bed outside cabins with balconies, 12 four-berth window cabins, 10 four-berth inside cabins, and 4 four-berth pet friendly window cabins. For passengers with impaired mobility there are 2 four-berth wide access outside cabins, and 2

The Little People's Play Area is well equipped to keep children entertained during the crossing. *(Miles Cowsill)*

The Niarbyl Lounge offers a fresh, relaxing environment with a colour palette based on coastal areas of the Island. *(Miles Cowsill)*

The spacious Bar makes strong use of natural light at the aft end of Deck 7. *(Steam Packet)*

four-berth wide access inside cabins. All cabins are ensuite and can accommodate up to 140 passengers in total.

The balcony cabins are a luxury feature not normally found on ferries around Britain; these cabins have a coffee machine and premium bathroom fittings. Interior finishes follow through from the public areas, with the shape of the flag in the carpet and little spots of heather colours to add warmth to these light and bright cabins.

Standard or pullman cabins have top bunks that can be pulled down, and bottom beds that convert into couches, enabling the cabin to accommodate passengers with babies and prams. The bathrooms are spacious

and, unusually for a ferry, the shower door is of glass. The interior layout of each cabin is optimised to incorporate a desk. These designs were tested with a variety of people to ensure that they could accommodate everyone in comfort. The pet-friendly cabins have been built with hard high-quality finishes to optimise their longevity.

The cabin deck area is fitted to cruise ship standard with doors set back from the corridor. The main carpet walkway is based on the heritage of the Laxey Mill and the Manx woollen trade, reflecting the weft and weave of tweeds and tartans, whilst incorporating the characteristic flash of red.

At the stern of the vessel lies the 145-passenger

The cabin area on Deck 8 features the artistic work of Megan Hindley. (*Miles Cowsill*)

The wide range of cabins will be welcomed by *Manxman*'s passengers. (*Steam Packet*)

The subtle decor of one of the large cabins on *Manxman*. *(Steam Packet)*

capacity Barrule Premium Lounge and the 61-passenger capacity Executive Club Lounge. Both offer a wide variety of furniture, with multiple seating opportunities from solo chairs to business desks, pullman seating, and sofas. Each has access to external seating spaces overlooking the stern. The twoLounges were designed to link the compass points on the Island, so furniture is laid out to reflect the relative geographic locations of elements of the island, linking everything together within that section. Access to both Lounges is by key card.

The Executive Club palette is based on the moorlands and heathlands, with a carpet mirroring the paths taken by the animals and humans across the landscape, with the very rich colours of heather, burnt heathland and stone walls with mosses and lichens. The lounge offers meeting spaces, as well as workstations for the business traveller, with a complimentary service of

The Executive Club Lounge *(Miles Cowsill)*

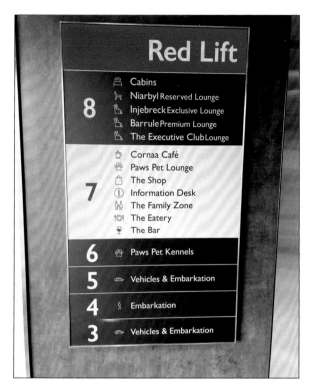

Clear signage gives passengers easy access around the ship. (*Miles Cowsill*)

Another stairwell mural illustrating the viking and transport heritage of the Island. (*Miles Cowsill*)

food and drink on offer. This premium experience is enhanced by quality light fittings and a softness to the bulkheads that builds a calming influence, and branding that reflects the three legs of Mann.

The Barrule Premium Lounge follows the same luxury specification, offering a toned-down approach, with the twin peaks of North and South Barrule prominent on the logo. The Lounge is brighter, with an eclectic mix of furniture. The theme here is the seasonality of woodland, with fresh green tints, autumn colours, and a carpet based on tree and rock lichen, with the signature tick of red.

DECK 9

The *Manxman's* crew will live on board the vessel for up to two weeks at a time, and the wellbeing of crew was identified as vitally important to the Steam Packet management team from the outset. The Company's brief for crew accommodation was to be of equivalent standard to that in the passenger areas. So, *Manxman's* crew will enjoy the use of a cinema room, gym, and a dedicated lounge area, with a separate officers' lounge, as on a cruise ship. Every member of crew has their own single cabin, the majority of which have an external window. These standards surpass the quality of crew facilities found on any passenger vessel around the UK.

From sketch to reality - the Injebreck Lounge as completed by the shipyard. *(Miles Cowsill)*

The Executive Club Lounge with art from Ellie Baker and Darren Jackson. *(Miles Cowsill)*

The outside deck area on Deck 7. *(Miles Cowsill)*

ENHANCING ENTERTAINMENT

The introduction of *Manxman* heralds a revolution in connectivity and entertainment for passengers. The Steam Packet selected Baze Technology - a renowned provider of Internet Protocol Television (IPTV) solutions – to transform passengers' onboard entertainment experience. The BazePort IPTV system is the industry leader in professional environments, and the company has been delivering IPTV solutions to customers across many industries worldwide since 2008, with their first customers in the offshore and maritime industries.

BazePort is designed to enable sustained meaningful interactions, regardless of where the system is deployed, operating 24 hours a day, seven days a week, in the most demanding of environments. The system is constantly updated with new and advanced functionality, so that installations can continue to stay abreast of the latest technology. The BazePort system provides users with a large choice of applications and functionality delivering a seamless entertainment experience with high-quality Live television, information and content, easy navigation, and reliable performance. The product is specifically designed to meet the needs of customers in remote or challenging locations. Currently, BazePort is in use with more than 80,000 units at around 800 installations all over the world.

The BazePort system on *Manxman* was tailored to meet the unique needs of the Steam Packet, which included 152 Philips professional televisions and a unique solution with a built-in BazePort native Android app. This solution eliminates the need for extra hardware, except for the television and an ethernet cable. The solution includes a wide range of functionality to ensure a high-quality user experience.

The features deployed on *Manxman* include live

The Executive Club Lounge features six fully-reclining pod seats. *(Steam Packet)*

television, radio, video on demand, and a cloud publishing service that allows for multiple video information channels to be published as television channels. There is also catch-up television functionality that allows passengers to access a programme archive and watch live recordings at their own convenience. The televisions are automatically muted when important messages or alarms are sent through the Public Address and General Alarm Systems. Additionally, the personal device entertainment feature lets passengers bring their own devices on board and access live television, movies, news, or listen to podcasts through the BazePort web application, as well as receive essential safety messages and access the Information Portal directly on their smartphone, tablet, or laptop.

With BazePort's reliable and user-friendly system, passengers, and crew on board *Manxman* will be able to stay entertained and informed throughout their journey.

6

island reflection
the art of
Manxman

SMC Design were appointed by the Steam Packet not only to design the internal layout of the ferry but also to curate a selection of art on board. Until the late eighties, very few ferry operators thought of producing specially commissioned artwork for their operations. The introduction of *Bretagne* by Brittany Ferries in 1989, saw the first vessel operating in British waters with a large selection of commissioned art on board, undertaken by the Scottish artist Alexander Goudie. Other ferry companies were quick to follow, as was the cruise industry. SMC Design have managed special commissions of artwork for Saga Cruises, Norwegian Cruise Lines, MSC and DFDS, to name a few.

SMC started work on the art aspects of the project some two years before the delivery of the vessel. Emmie Ratter led the art project for *Manxman* with the Isle of Man Arts Council, which overall has provided a selection of unique paintings, photography, and sculpture. Emmie is an islander herself; she was brought up on Shetland, studied History of Art at the University of Glasgow, and later undertook an MLitt (Master of Letters) focusing on museum and private collecting and collection practices. Her first job was with the V&A Museum in London and after spending three years in Japan she took up an appointment in the

Bruno Cavellec

Amy Bourbon

art department of IMC Design. Emmie has enjoyed all the aspects of her work with this commission, especially visiting the Isle of Man and discovering the wealth of artistic talent on the Island.

As passengers walk around the two passenger decks they will discover many pieces of outstanding art from the fifteen commissioned artists – their work will bring something extra and a chance to escape from today's busy world.

ADAM BERRY

Adam is a local artist with a background in animation and the Art Foundation at Isle of Man College Library (UCM). He went to school at St Ninian's in Douglas and later studied at the Isle of Man College. Adam's work is very popular on the Island, and he has designed logos for organisations, posters, prints and architectural drawings of iconic Manx buildings. Graphic is probably the best way to describe his art style. His early inspirations came from reading stories of

Jinny the Witch. Recent work of his can be found around the Island, including along the seafront at Ramsey and the Victory Cafe on the TT Course.

AMY BOURBON

Amy is a fine artist specialising in painting and drawing. She was brought up in Buckinghamshire and now lives in the north of the Island, just outside Ramsey. After leaving school she obtained her PhD from Birmingham Institute of Art and Design. Her artwork involves large-scale oil paintings inspired by the places that she has encountered. She uses a layering technique to develop depth, giving the impression of space alongside intricate detail. She has a great passion for islands and has recently been commissioned to do work in Jersey. Two of her favourite locations in the Isle of Man are Laxey and Ramsey.

ANDREW MACKELLAR

Andrew moved to the Isle of Man nearly 40 years ago, a place he was familiar with and loved, having married a Manx girl. He lives in the south of the Island close to some of his favourite places, Langness and Fort Island. Though land and seascapes have formed most of his work over the last 40 years, in the most recent decade his paintings have become more abstract in nature. The intention to convey aspects of the natural environment remains, without being specifically representative. Andrew's paintings and drawings show a fascination for natural forms, their

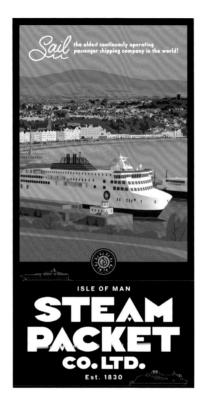

Adam Berry

structures and placement: stone circles, neolithic, and iron age sites have been an inspiration to him in recent years. His paintings for *Manxman* are in pen and ink and have a distinctive quality to them, mixing accurate representation and an abstract impressionism to convey a sense of a life.

ANNA CLUCAS

Anna was brought up in the Isle of Man and attended the Isle of Man College in Douglas, which is now known as the UCM. Anna graduated with a BA (Hons) from the University of Wolverhampton in 2000, and has been involved in many exhibitions, both internationally and locally. Anna teaches art and

Andrew Mackellar in his studio at Castletown

Anna Clucas

design at the UCM, the Isle of Man prison, and runs Art Tank at Kensington Arts, an art space for young people. Today she finds inspiration for her bold and expressive oil paintings in the environments surrounding her. Driven by creative expression and the exploration of colour and shape through synaesthesia, Anna's paintings on *Manxman* have been inspired by the music and lyrics from local folk, cross-over punk metal, darkwave/gothic bands, the Ballaghs, Mark E Moon, Alice Dudley, and Swarf Damage, from the Island.

BRUNO CAVELLEC

Bruno was born in the western Breton city of Quimper, in France, and started his early career in Paris. A self-taught artist and illustrator, he moved to England after meeting Jill, now his wife. After enjoying life in Rugby, and some early successes with exhibitions at the RBSA in Birmingham and some other regional galleries, they decided to relocate to the Isle of Man, which would prove to be a positive move for Bruno, allowing him to expand his interest in music and art. Atmosphere, mood and colour are the key ingredients of his oil paintings, with multiple layers of gesso, paint and soil featuring in the more abstract and experimental canvases. After some 12 years in Peel, he has been able to pursue his dream and finally release his first music album. His artwork captures the open star-studded skies and features a Manx family (the Quirk's from the sunset city) standing on rock pools behind Peel Castle.

Darren Jackson

Stephanie Quayle

DARREN JACKSON AND STEPHANIE QUAYLE

Darren was born in Sunderland in 1974 and studied model making and design with first degree honours. He then went on to work in London, in model making and special effects and as an ice sculptor, which led to him competing in international competitions and symposiums representing the UK and the Isle of Man. Meanwhile, his partner was brought up in the Isle of Man on a farm just outside the village of St Mark's. Stephanie graduated from the Royal College of Art in London with an MA in Fine Art Sculpture.

Stephanie and Darren have been responsible for

Ellie Baker

some well-known and instantly recognisable large-scale sculptures around the Island, including the Bull for the Southern Show centenary, made from old bits of farm machinery, the giant elk at the Wildlife Park and the bronze 'when I grow up' sculpture outside the RNLI shop in Ramsey.

ELLIE BAKER

Ellie is a landscape painter with a Foundation Diploma in Fine Art from Central Saint Martin's College of Art and Design, London. Her distinct style draws the viewer in and sets the imagination to work and combines many elements from the local rural land and seascapes. To create her pieces for *Manxman*, she started with a layer of ground on the canvas to provide a textured base. She then applied a warm and rich palette of acrylics reflecting both the landscapes of the Isle of Man and the experiences of islanders and visitors. The larger work depicts an iconic prospect as seen when approaching by sea, resonating with lines written by the Manx poet T.E. Brown. The hillscape is lined with a lustrous gold, reflecting the outstanding beauty to be discovered here. Her second piece is semi-abstract, with a bold application of paint which instils a sense of place and identity, capturing a moment of interaction between the Island and the sea and sky that surround it.

Graham Rider in his studio

GRAHAM RIDER

Graham comes originally from London, where he went to art colleges in Southend, Norwich, and Cambridge to develop his career. His first real job, after sixth form, was in the centre of London in the civil service, and at lunchtime he used to walk to the National Gallery to discover his interest in art. He moved to the Island from Norfolk in 2016, which has allowed him to develop his particular interest in coast, mountains, and landscapes. Since moving he particularly found a great love for the Ayres in the north of the Isle of Man. He has been a painter for over 40 years, most of that time has been spent painting beach and landscapes. Like many artists he has had various exhibitions and commissions, including Railtrack for their boardroom at Liverpool Street Station.

IAN COULSON

Ian was born and brought up in the city of Peel, and after attending art school on the Island went to the UK to further develop his art education. On his return to the Isle of Man he started to learn Manx and took part in the confident flowering of a new Manx culture, and politics, that occurred in the 1970s and 80s. He earned money fishing and fish curing, which allowed

Ian Coulson

him to continue his interest in making art. In later life he became the foundation course tutor at the Isle of Man College, and many of the other artists' work on *Manxman* have been influenced by his thoughts, and teaching of the importance of maintaining and developing our Manx cultural identity.

Ian's interests range from paintings of the back streets of Douglas, which have provided lifelong subject matter, to his fascination with his grandfather's life as a Hull trawlerman, who

Jacqui Mulvagh

had spent his working life off Iceland and the north coast of Norway in the Barents Sea trawling for cod. Ian researched how the Admiralty had requisitioned trawlers for minesweepers, and their crews volunteering 'en masse' to go into this dangerous work became compulsively fascinating for him. This led to a major group of large drawings, made on Admiralty charts, telling of the travails of trawlers and their crews, and their companions the sea birds of the North Atlantic. These covered the floors of St Germain's Cathedral. This work has influenced his thinking, about the pictures he has done for *Manxman* and of the Steam Packet's involvement in the evacuation of Dunkirk in the Second World War.

JACQUI MULVAGH

Jacqui is a former graphic designer who later turned to become a self-taught illustrator. Drawing fills her day, when her time isn't taken up with her four kids, husband, two cats and the dog!

Ever since she was little, she has had a big imagination, frequently seeing characters in shapes on walls or in shadows. Characters are a big part of what she creates today. Feeling connected, loved, and happy is important to her. She moved to the Isle of Man some years ago and today has a busy life with art, and her family, and has recently opened a café in Onchan where she will be able to exhibit her works but also teach art to future artists.

JADE BOYLAN

Jade was born and raised in the Isle of Man, after leaving school she studied for a BA in Fine Art from University College Isle of Man and Liverpool John Moore's University. As an artist and designer, she works freelance full time from her home in the north of the Island. Her colourful and playful designs have been stocked in shops all over the world, including Top Shop, ASOS, Selfridges, Nordstrom, and Anthropologie. Her distinctive work on *Manxman* will be displayed in the Paws Lounge area. Jade is passionate about the Isle of Man and Manx culture and is also a member of the Isle of Man Arts Council.

Jade Boylan

Megan Hindley

Megan Hindley

MEGAN HINDLEY

Megan was brought up in the Isle of Man, attended Castle Rushen school and then went to the art college in Douglas. After working in Wales and London she returned to the Island to expand her interest in art, studying mankind and the natural world: nearly all her work reflects this, from small tattoo flash drawings to large-scale murals on the sides of buildings. She likes to play with humour within her pieces, capturing an emotion or facial expression in moments of terror or laughter. Line quality and contrast are important to her. She will usually paint with ink and brush, but she recently tried charcoals. Megan has 19 pieces of art on *Manxman*.

RON STRATHDEE

Ron was brought up in Scotland and attended Grangemouth High School. He then went to sea on tankers for 13 years and came ashore in 1987 to work in an officer recruitment office for a major oil company. He moved to the Island in 1982 after getting married and then worked for the Isle of Man Ship Registry from 1997. After his move in 1987 he re-

Ron Strathdee.

Sally Black

discovered the enjoyment of photography, and the later development of digital photography allowed him to expand his interests. He loves the Island, with its varied and magnificent landscapes. Like every photographer he has a favourite vista that he likes to visit regularly, but he admits to being spoilt for choice. He especially loves night-time photography and the Northern Lights, which are extremely beautiful with the Island's outstanding Dark Skies. Not only has he worked with Steam Packet on this project, but he has helped produce a set of stamps for the Isle of Man Post Office.

SALLY BLACK

From the age of ten Sally lived in Castletown, then Port St Mary, and after schooling attended the Isle of Man College for a Foundation in Art. After many years in the United States, she now lives in Peel overlooking the bay, with wonderful views of Peel Castle and the distant Mull of Galloway. She fondly remembers ferry crossings and many of her family members, from deckhands to captain, were Steam Packet men. Originally a scientific illustrator in New York and Virginia, she started exhibiting in 2009 and her works are in collections all over the world. Her first sold painting can be seen in the Little Fish restaurant on the quay in Douglas.

Sally today expresses her love for the natural world through her oil paintings on large-scale canvases, but she also paints on pottery produced by her husband. Much of her work has been influenced by the colours of Bali, as she is a regular visitor to Indonesia.

Her love of nature is expressed in the two large paintings 'Beneath the Bows' in the Niarbyl Reserved Lounge on *Manxman*, which depict many of the fish native to the Irish Sea.

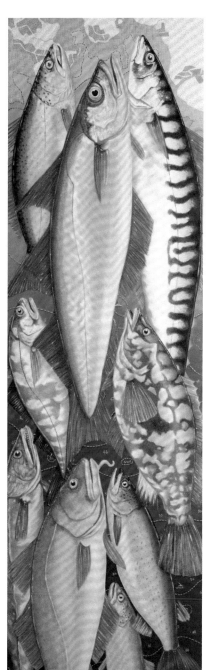

Sally Black

SMC Design Team

CHAPTER SEVEN

FROM
BUILD
TO DELIVERY

In autumn 2019, the Steam Packet issued a tender to shipyards around the world, inviting expressions of interest to build the new bespoke vessel. There was an encouraging response from a range of specialist shipbuilders, which the team reviewed and assessed to whittle the selection down. Houlder provided technical background and support in reviewing these proposals to enable the Company to make an informed decision on the choice of builder. Affinity (Shipping) LLP brought shipbroking, research, and advisory services to the project, with Nick Wood and Nick Pugh assisting the Company through the tendering process, providing advice on environmentally friendly propulsion systems and fuels, the shortlisting of shipyards, and contract negotiations. They continued to support the project and brought guidance and assistance during post contract discussions.

The senior management team began a series of visits to shortlisted shipyards in February 2020. There were a huge number of factors to take into consideration and the approach had to be thorough to ensure the most suitable shipbuilder was selected. These shipyard visits played an important part in this process. The number of bidders was gradually reduced from 21 to a short list of two – Remontowa of Poland and Hyundai Mipo of South Korea. Evaluation of the latter was initially hindered by the remoteness of the yard, exacerbated by emerging pandemic travel restrictions, but eventually quarantine requirements were clarified, and shipyard visits proved possible.

After months of extensive evaluation, discussion and deliberation, the Directors decided in July 2020 that the new vessel would be constructed at the Hyundai Mipo Dockyard (HMD) in South Korea. The selected builder is a leading blue-chip shipyard with a proven track record of delivering vessels on time, to budget and to trademark high standards.

HMD was founded in 1975 and established itself as one of the world's leading dockyards dedicated to the construction of mid-sized vessels. The shipyard is equipped with an integrated information system that spans the complete manufacturing process, with an advanced design and engineering system backed by extensive research and development facilities. HMD is a leader in the eco-friendly ship market, utilising the world's top eco-ship technology.

The *Manxman* construction contract was particularly important for HMD, as it represented the first European ro-pax project for the company and a significant milestone in the shipyard's history. The successful construction and delivery of a quality vessel offered the company's passenger ship division an opportunity to expand business further into the European market.

HMD already had a strong reputation in the specialised building of commercial vessels, such as product/chemical tankers, gas carriers, and container carriers. The *Manxman* contract was more challenging in building a passenger ship to European standards. The company had delivered several ro-pax vessels for the domestic Korean market, but the specification laid down for *Manxman* was to a significantly higher standard than HMD had previously encountered. The construction and completion of the ship's accommodation sections was to prove especially tough, but the help of the Steam Packet personnel and the local support team on site proved invaluable in ensuring a quality delivery. Moreover, importing materials and equipment from a variety of European countries during the COVID-19 pandemic proved particularly challenging, but active management of the procurement plan ensured these difficulties were minimised.

HMD's team were to spend some 192,000-man

Above and below: Each of the key construction milestones was appropriately recorded at the shipyard. *(HMD)*

Below: The *Manxman*'s bulbous bow, ready for fitting to the vessel. *(HMD)*

hours working on the design of *Manxman*, and a further 286,000-man hours on the shipyard construction phase. These figures exclude the time spent by subcontractors on the project. Building *Manxman* absorbed 16,200 pieces of piping, 5,274 tonnes of steel, and 468,045 meters of cable.

Constructing *Manxman* so far from the Isle of Man required the assistance of local specialists to help support the build and delivery process. The team in South Korea included project management company Sea Quest Marine (SQM) who helped oversee construction in the shipyard. The company was established in 2003 and employs a team of over 200 specialists in the major shipyards in Asia. SQM provided independent on-site supervision and advice to the Steam Packet team on the specialist areas of the build process, including welding inspections, pipe production and testing, paint preparation and application, electrical and machinery installation, culminating in support during the testing and trials process. Founder and CEO, Janne Anderson, was project manager of the SQM team at the HMD yard. As a former technical director at Star Cruises and Norwegian Cruise Lines, he brought considerable familiarity with the high-end passenger vessels that the project was looking to emulate.

With the project commencing in 2020, coronavirus travel restrictions presented several additional obstacles, with limited potential for on-site visits, and disruptions to typical communication lines – exacerbated by the eight-hour time difference between the UK and South Korea. These obstacles were overcome by Houlder by adjusting how the team conveyed complex points to the Hyundai MIPO team, to avoid ambiguity, as well as exploring new channels through which project discussions could take place.

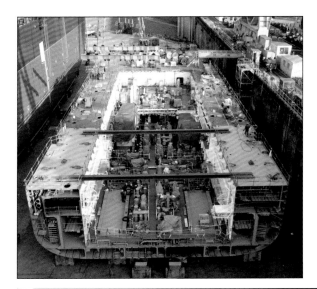

The *Manxman* was built in sections and assembled at the shipyard. *(HMD)*

A rare view of the hull cross-section, as the Wärtsilä engines are craned into place. *(Steam Packet)*

The hull of **Manxman** alongside in the assembly dock. *(HMD)*

Steady hand required! The completed bridge section is craned onto the hull as part of the assembly process. *(HMD)*

The *Manxman* is assembled from a kit of sections, built independently and brought together in the construction dock. *(HMD)*

The completed funnel and crew accommodation section is craned on board. *(HMD)*

All vehicle traffic will access *Manxman* through the stern door, here seen in the process of being fitted. *(HMD)*

A kick off meeting took place at the HMD Head Office in South Korea on Tuesday 17th August 2021, ahead of the commencement of *Manxman's* construction. Representatives from the Steam Packet were joined by the HMD Project Team, Houlder Naval Architects, Sea Quest Marine Project Management, and Health, Safety and Environment and Quality Assurance. The meeting ensured that all parties shared an understanding of the importance of the scope, goals, budget, and the project timeline.

The *Manxman's* formal construction commenced three days later on Friday 20th August 2021, with the detailed design of the vessel – comprising of a total of around 300 detailed plans – complete. This significant milestone – known as the steel cutting ceremony – took place at the HMD shipyard in Ulsan, with the pushing of a button to initiate the cutting of the first piece of steel. Plasma files produced from the approved construction drawings were used to direct the shipyard's plate cutting machines to cut each section of the vessel automatically and accurately. The sections of the vessel, known as blocks, were constructed by welding together the cut plates ready to be blasted and painted.

By December more than 80% of *Manxman's* blocks had been constructed and were either in the process of being painted or at the pre-outfitting stage, for the installation of cable trays, pipes, and ducting. The build process could only commence when all the blocks were complete.

The second major milestone was marked on Friday 24th December 2021 in the keel-laying ceremony, which traditionally invites good luck to the construction of a ship and throughout her life. Covid-19 restrictions prevented a 1979 coin - marking the Millennium of Tynwald and presented to the Company by the Isle of Man Treasury Minister - reaching the shipyard in time for the ceremony, so the Chief Executive of the build team generously provided a hugely sentimental replacement coin for use in the ceremony. This marked the beginning of the formal build of the vessel at Ulsan. The first of 36 blocks - weighing 215 tonnes -that formed part of the forward engine room were laid in dry dock number 4. Two further blocks then joined the first in the dock, enabling the welding and connecting works to commence.

By January 2022, *Manxman's* build was progressing quickly, with more than 110,000-man hours (or 4,583-man days) having been expended on construction. The four main generator engines were delivered from Wärtsila in Finland and installed into the engine rooms, along with other large items of machinery including sewage treatment plants and the main switchboards. The vessel has reached her full length, and construction at the forward end stretched up to deck 5 (the upper car deck) of the nine covered decks. This rapid progress enabled *Manxman* to be floated for the first time in April 2022.

Erection of the accommodation superstructure was completed in May 2022. The 400-tonne aft accommodation block – the largest on the vessel – had already tested the upper limit of the shipyard cranes.

FITTING OUT MANXMAN

The important task of delivering the quality of interior outfitting of *Manxman* so that the final product matched the ambition of the design was entrusted to Sejin Technical Industries Co. Ltd., Korea, led by the company's President Minseok Jang

The company is a leading interior manufacturer of prefabricated cabins, ceiling panels, wall panels, internal doors, wet units, and customisable marine furniture made in wood, steel, and aluminium honeycomb. Sejin specialises in this role for all types of ships and offshore

structures, with an extensive portfolio encompassing interior design services, engineering, fabrication, supply, installation, testing, and commissioning of new ship builds, conversions, and refits.

The company has over three decades' experience in providing global turnkey solutions for interior outfitting to leading megaprojects constructed across Asia. Over this period, Sejin has built a dynamic organisation with more than 300 employees, established three fully owned production factories in Korea, and successfully obtained ISO 9001, ISO 14001, and ISO 45001 certification by DNV GL. Sejin's strong track record and sound corporate finances have established the company as a crucial integrated partner for all the major Korean shipyards.

The scope of work for the *Manxman* project included the design, engineering, fabrication, supply, installation, testing, and commissioning of all cabins and public areas on the vessel. This totalled some 7,280 square meters of space, covering 42 passenger cabins, 95 public spaces, and accommodation for 52 crew members. The remit required compliance with European interior standards and practices, so Sejin engaged a procurement team based in Busan, Korea, who visited Europe many times to identify and carefully select the most experienced suppliers for this crucial element of the project.

The team worked closely with leading specialist European manufacturing partners with skills in producing accommodation materials for cruise and ro-pax ferry projects, particularly for furnishing and seating, flooring, carpeting, doors, and decorative lighting. The installation team collaborated with installation supervisors from their European partners to ensure that all finishes were completed to the high standard required by the contract. And, by choosing European suppliers, Sejin ensured that quick and easy post contract services

Close liaison between teams at the shipyard ensured a timely quality delivery. (HMD)

will be available locally for decades to come.

Sejin approached Estonian Marine and Manufacturing Initiative (EMI) - a network of manufacturers and service providers in Estonia - to support the interior material fit out for *Manxman*. The two organisations have a long-standing working relationship. EMI, led by Argo Sildvee, offer a high-end value chain supplier network bespoke to individual projects, delivered in an open book manner that ensures full transparency throughout the project.

EMI selected several specialist manufacturers from Estonia during the interior mock-up phase, with Velvet Engineering providing the engineering and technical drawings for the fit-out. SunShip manufactured furniture for the cabins and public areas, whilst Divasoft supplied sofas and beds. Marmi Futerno provided stone works by and Repston were selected to supply metalwork and public area tables. EMI undertook the pre-lamination works for the Fipro panels by PlaatDetail and these panels were installed to each of *Manxman's* walls.

Manufacture in Estonia created a significant

challenge for local logistics specialists CF&S to deliver the completed items to South Korea. Some 23 x 40-ft and 9 x 20-ft containers were packed with the ready-made furniture and components, with a further 11 air shipments of materials from the EU, UK and USA totalling 35,200 kg in weight.

Remarkably, the Estonian team were able to complete the manufacture of all these items without sending a single person to Ulsan for meetings or approvals. A strong communication system was established so that the Estonian companies manufactured all the goods and Sejin were able to complete the installation at the MIPO shipyard. This was only achieved through the employment of a state-of-the-art technical drawing approval system that encompassed 3D images to eliminate problems during the installation phase.

Teams from the Steam Packet, Sejin, and SMC Design visited the worksites in Estonia to formulate an Inspection and Test Plan (ITP) before the main deliveries were despatched. This enabled trust to be established at an early point in the production process and give confidence that the furniture installed in *Manxman* was going to meet the demanding specification and quality standards. The ITP process gave the green light to all the parties involved, confirming that preparatory work had been completed correctly and making installation at the HMD shipyard in Ulsan straightforward. The smoothness of this process was reflected in a low reclamation rate of less than 2% for the entire ship, illustrating the strengths of EMI's approach and quality standards for an installation on the other side of the world.

Despite the widespread disruptions to global shipping and supply chain caused by the war in Ukraine, the project team successfully executed all the interior

Finishing touches are applied to **Manxman**'s twin controllable pitch propellers. *(HMD)*

The funnel section is inched into place. *(HMD)*

A busy shipyard! **Manxman** lies alongside the tanker **Dee 4 Mahogany**. *(HMD)*

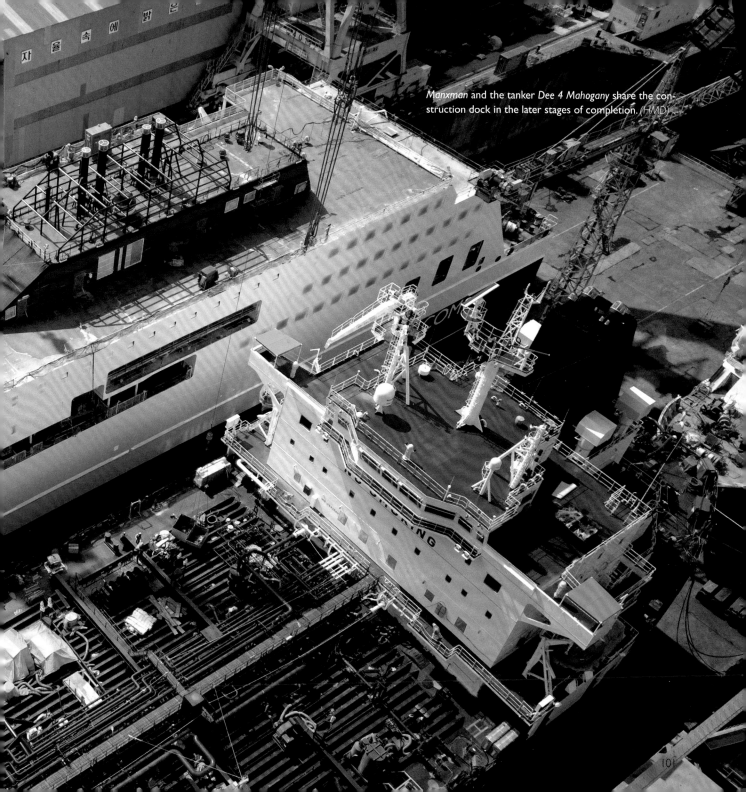

Manxman and the tanker *Dee 4 Mahogany* share the construction dock in the later stages of completion. *(HMD)*

Left: A proud moment as *Manxman* is towed from the construction dock at the Ulsan shipyard on 16th June 2022. *(HMD)*

Above: The bulbous bow is prominent in this view from the construction dock as work continues on the bridge section. *(HMD)*

The **Manxman** is eased out of the construction dock at Ulsan on 16th June 2022. *(HMD)*

Tugs hold **Manxman** steady as she exits the dock. *(HMD)*

outfitting works in accordance with the agreed quality standards outlined in the main contract.

Building at a Korean shipyard created new challenges in ensuring that onboard facilities met standards appropriate to the UK rather than the Asian domestic market. Accessibility requirements in the Korean domestic market are less prescriptive than those in the UK so, for example, door sills that might require a 200mm ramp in Korea have to be evened out for the UK market; this has a significant impact on the design. There is no consensus in Korea on which way light switches are designed to operate, so ensuring that they are all installed in the same way imposed a different way of working on the shipyard team.

The *Manxman* was floated at around 08:30, Korean time, on Tuesday 14th June 2022, marking another major milestone in her build; the HMD shipyard had kept to the schedule set out two years previously despite Covid-19, travel restrictions and closed borders. After successfully performing leakage checks *Manxman* was taken by tugs to an outfitting berth for the internal works to continue. These included electrical works, the commissioning of machinery and equipment, and the outfitting of interior spaces. A formal ceremony was attended by representatives of the Steam Packet site team and shipyard management. H D Shin, President and CEO of HMD presented Jim Royston, Fleet Operations Manager and Project Manager from the Steam Packet, with the official certificate of launching.

The first generator on *Manxman* was started at 14:30 Korean time, (06:30 UK time), on Thursday 25th August 2022 by Senior Chief Engineer Dean Ellis, who pressed the start button to successfully fire up the engine at the first time of asking. The three other generators later also started without problems. Safety protection devices were next to be tested, ahead of the starting of powering of

The team poses for the camera ahead of the launch of *Manxman*. *(HMD)*

Work in progress on the aft end facilities on deck 7. *(HMD)*

Seating in the Niarbyl Lounge is protected from damage during the build phase. *(HMD)*

Congratulations to Steam-Packet with the Manxman

3 x person elevator & 1 Dumbwaiter delivered by
Lift Emotion ⌐ www.lift-emotion.com

Tailormade solutions for
your marine projects

+ Estonian Shipbuilding since
  750 AD (1260 years)

+ ManxMan no.1 furniture
  manufacturer and supplier

Estonian Marine and Manufacturing Initiative

⊕ www.emi.com.ee
✉ info@emi.com.ee
📱 + 372 5596 9121

the vessel's switchboard, and the commissioning of the power management systems. Finally, *Manxman's* propulsion systems were tested.

In September, storm Hinnamnor brought 90mph winds to South Korea, the eighth-strongest typhoon in the country's history. The Hyundai Mipo shipyard had contingency plans in place to handle extreme weather, moving vessels with propulsion systems out to sea, and applying additional lines and fenders to those such as *Manxman* that had to remain at the outfitting berth. Fortunately, *Manxman* suffered only superficial cosmetic damage, which was quickly rectified.

The Houlder team undertook regular visits to the shipyard during this construction period and worked with the SeaQuest team to ensure that delivery quality matched the design specification. All the hard work came together during the sea trials that began on Saturday 10th December 2022, when the naval architecture input was tested against output lightweight, vessel stability, speed, and power output, whilst observing the efficacy of the stabilisers and the levels of noise and vibration around the vessel. The *Manxman* was put through her paces, and the testing exposed a gearbox issue that required rectification. Far better to find out at this stage, with the shipyard able to initiate a repair programme with the gearbox manufacturer.

The *Manxman* remained well within the contractual delivery agreement date and, following repairs to the gearbox, the vessel returned to sea from Ulsan on her final set of sea trials on Wednesday 12th April 2023. This exhaustive test of all the vessel's systems was passed with flying colours, and the *Manxman* triumphantly returned to Ulsan, ready to be handed over to the Steam Packet.

Steam Packet Chairman Lars Ugland picks up the story of the naming and delivery ceremonies.

The *Manxman* on sea trials off the Korean coast. *(Steam Packet)*

NAMING CEREMONY WEDNESDAY 3RD MAY 2023

Guests were taken to the Hyundai shipyard office to watch a video of the shipyard and milestones from the first shipyard in the group Hyundai Heavy Industries, which began operations in 1975.

After the video, Geraldine was asked to perform a dummy run of reading the ritual of naming the vessel and then cutting the rope with an axe, which sets off the streamers and fireworks. This worked on her first try. On the way out of the office, we were lined up for a photoshoot. There were several cameramen snapping away all day at every turn.

We moved from the office to the berth where Manxman was moored. Traditionally, the sponsor or the Godmother naming the vessel is the most important person on the day, so Geraldine and I were taken in a limousine escorted by a motorbike with siren and emergency lights; following us was another limousine with the Group Vice Chairman & CEO, Mr Sam H Ka and the CEO/President of Hyundai Mipo Dockyard, Mr H K Kim and Mr C J Youn, Executive Vice President of the Design Office. The rest of the group followed in a coach.

We entered the podium and were seated whilst Mr H K Kim

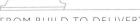

Cause for celebration! The formal handover of *Manxman* is applauded by (L-R) Janne Andersson (MD of Sea Quest Marine), Jim Royston, Lars Ugland, Geraldine Ugland, Mr HR Kim (President and CEO of HMD), KR Baek, JH Choi, and Ryan Choi. *(HMD)*

and I gave speeches. This was followed by Geraldine cutting the rope with a ceremonial axe, which opened the ball with streamers and set off the fireworks.

We moved to the next podium where we witnessed the naming of the vessel and the traditional smashing of a bottle of champagne against the vessel's side for good luck and safety for the officers and crew sailing on her. This tradition might go back to ancient times and might have originated in Greece. However, it was not champagne in those days but some form of alcoholic drink. In Scotland they use Scotch Whiskey even today.

After the naming there were several line ups for more photos. When all that was finished, we headed onboard Manxman, where we started a guided tour on Deck 7. We moved up and around Deck 8 before we entered Deck 9 to be shown the instruments, navigation, and communication equipment on the bridge. It is a

very large bridge compared to the equipment mounted there. We then lined up to cut a ribbon to commission the vessel's bridge. Each one of us was given a pair of scissors to cut the ribbon simultaneously. We were also invited to sound the vessels horn with two short and one long blast. This took some time with every person and couples jointly participating from both the shipyard and the Steam Packet guests.

We took the lift down to Deck 3, the lower car deck; those interested in the engine room were invited down a further deck. I have always enjoyed visiting engine rooms and I was accompanied by a good number of the guests including a few ladies. The exit from the vessel is through the pilot side door on Deck 3. Limousines and a coach were waiting to take us to the shipyard guesthouse where we were met by more photographers.

Champagne and canapes were served in a large open space,

Geraldine Ugland prepares to name **Manxman** with the traditional bottle of champagne. (HMD)

surrounded by guesthouse buildings, whilst a group of four Korean musicians played and sang Korean traditional music. After about 45 minutes we were guided towards the dining room where lunch was to be served. However, on the way we were again asked to line up for more photos in various groups, and one group with only women.

A large gong at the entrance to the lunchroom was set up for the Godmother to hit for everyone to proceed into the next room where the lunch would be served. Geraldine hit the gong three times and the last massive strike of the gong is still ringing in my ears...

At the end of a delicious lunch, we were shown a video of the building of the Manxman from the first steel cutting till completion. This was followed by a speech by Mr Sam H Ka, who toasted all the guests and wished the Manxman good luck as well as to the owners. I was then asked to propose a toast.

Traditionally, this can go to anyone person or group of persons. I dedicated my toast to the crew of Manxman, and I included everyone that had been involved in the arrangement for the lunch. Then followed an exchange of gifts.

We were then taken back to our hotel.

DELIVERY CEREMONY WEDNESDAY 10TH MAY 2023

Between the naming ceremony and the delivery, Geraldine and I went to Japan for other business and returned to Korea on 9th May. Lots of minor works were carried out during that week onboard the Manxman.

On the day of the delivery 10th May, we again met at the shipyard office to finalise the extra cost of the vessel for additional work that the Steam Packet had commissioned. Any deduction or

A team celebration. Guests at the naming ceremony and a pristine **Manxman**. *(HMD)*

penalties the shipyard must pay is negotiated and entered into the final document, which is the Protocol of Delivery and Acceptance. Jim Royston, Janne Andersson, the CEO of our supervision company SeaQuest and I negotiated with Mr Chang-Jun Youn, Executive VP, Design Office, and Mr K R Baek, Senior Officer and Head of Contract Management Department. We spent five hours coming to a final agreement on cost.

The next morning on Thursday 11th May at 11.40 am, we signed the Protocol of Delivery and Acceptance, and Manxman was

transferred from Hyundai Mipo Dockyard to become the newest member of the Steam Packet fleet. Mr H K Kim, CEO and President signed on behalf of HMD, and I signed on behalf of the Steam Packet. We were then offered a glass of champagne and some other token gifts were exchanged, including the ceremonial pens.

The vessel was then placed in the charge of Senior Master Andy Atkinson and Chief Engineer Dean Ellis to make the final preparations for the departure on the long journey to the Isle of Man two days later.

Reflecting on the moment, Jim Royston, Fleet Operations Manager, and project manager for the *Manxman* build said: "It has been an honour to be involved in this landmark investment for the Company and the island. It is a testament to the hard work of everyone involved that *Manxman* has gone from a design on a computer screen to a completed vessel in less than two years." He added, "It has been a pleasure working with the team at Hyundai Mipo, our site supervision team Sea Quest Marine, naval architects Houlder's, insurers Lloyd's Register and most importantly the officers and crew of the Isle of Man Steam Packet Company who have been on site since the block erection stage."

As well as the team on site in South Korea, the build was supported by staff across the Company in the Isle of Man, and many other organisations such as the Isle of Man Ship Registry, the Red Ensign Group of British Shipping Registers, insurance companies, legal professionals, and the Isle of Man Government's Treasury Department, amongst many others. others. An estimated 1.2 million man-hours work had been expended on the project.

Managing Director Brian Thomson added "This is the first new build vessel the Company has commissioned since *Ben-my-Chree* joined the fleet in 1998, so the culmination of the build phase really is a seminal moment for everyone involved. A lot of hard work has gone into achieving this milestone and it's certainly a time to celebrate that. As the build phase ends, we now turn the focus to delivering *Manxman* to the Irish Sea and begin the process of getting her ready for service. There's the small matter of over 10,000 sea miles, approximately 23 days at sea and six different ports of call before *Manxman* arrives in UK waters. Our crew are excited about having the chance to handle the

Senior Master Andy Atkinson and Geraldine Ugland on the bridge of **Manxman**. *(HMD)*

newest ship in the fleet, and the voyage will give them a great opportunity to get to know *Manxman* and we're sure they'll do us proud."

Andy Atkinson is presented with a framed painting by Mr HK Kim to commemorate the naming of **Manxman**. *(HMD)*

STEAM PACKET MANXMAN TEAM

The Steam Packet project team directly involved in the planning, design and construction of the Manxman included: -

JIM ROYSTON, FLEET OPERATIONS MANAGER & MANXMAN PROJECT MANAGER

Jim started his career at sea in 1992 as an Engineer Cadet with Shell Shipping & Maritime, and then as Second Engineer on multidisciplinary research vessels with the Natural Environment Research Council, where he stayed for four years.

In 2002 he joined the Steam Packet, initially as Second Engineer and then Chief Engineer, sailing on several flagship vessels including *Ben-my-Chree*, *Lady of Mann*, *SeaCat Isle of Man* (later renamed *Sea Express 1* and

Senior Chief Engineer Dean Ellis and his team. *(Steam Packet)*

Snaefell), *SuperSeaCat Two* (later renamed *Viking*), *Emeraude France*, and *Manannan*. He was also part of the project teams for the rebuild of *Snaefell* in 2007 and renovation of the *Manannan* in 2008.

As Project Manager for the design and construction of *Manxman*, Jim was responsible for the timely delivery of the project; ensuring it stayed on track within the projected timeframe, and to budget. Some of his wide-ranging responsibilities included: -

- Reporting to the Company Board of Directors at every stage of the project
- Offering his expertise on the vessel outline specification and concept design during the initial phases
- Reviewing shipyard tenders and helping to shortlist potential yards
- Analysing the strengths, weaknesses, capabilities, and reliabilities of each yard as part of the shipyard inspection team
- Involvement in technical and contract

David Wing (Houlder), Dean Ellis, Jim Royston and Guy Prescodd in the drydock. *(Steam Packet)*

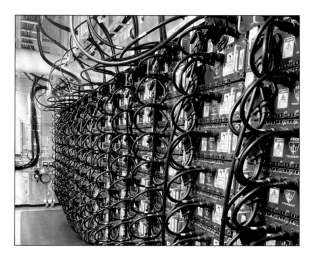

One of the battery units on **Manxman**. *(Miles Cowsill)*

One of the main Wärtsilä generator engines. *(Miles Cowsill)*

The main control panel in the Engine Room of **Manxman.** *(Miles Cowsill)*

discussions at the Seoul head offices prior to contract signing

- Liaising with the shipyard, classification society, flag administration, naval architects, and others throughout the detailed design stage, including plan approval

- Holding regular meetings with the design team to ensure the vessel design is as per the Steam Packet Company's requirements, the project is on schedule, to budget and all rules and regulations are adhered to.

Once construction began in August 2021, Jim regularly visited the HMD Shipyard for project update meetings, technical discussions, work inspections and keeping up to date with the on-site supervision team.

ANDY ATKINSON, SENIOR MASTER – MANXMAN

Andy began his career at sea in 2006 as a Deck Cadet with Maersk, sailing on tankers, container ships and ro-ro vessels. He moved to Carnival UK shortly after completing his cadetship, sailing on Cunard and P&O vessels as First Officer and Safety Officer respectively.

In 2015, he joined the Steam Packet as Chief Officer on *Ben-my-Chree* and *Manannan*, before being promoted to Master in 2018. Andy brought a wealth of experience and knowledge of technologies used in the modern passenger vessel industry. He assisted with plan approvals and the detailed design of *Manxman*, with a particular focus on the bridge layout, equipment, and mooring decks. Other key responsibilities included liaising with the ship's crew for their input and with regulatory bodies for radio licenses and registrations.

Andy was part of the on-site team at HMD Shipyard, acting as the Steam Packet Company's eyes and ears to ensure the vessel was built to the agreed specification and the satisfaction of regulatory bodies, reporting back to the Project Manager on a regular basis. He worked four weeks-on, four weeks-off, back-to-back.

DEAN ELLIS, SENIOR CHIEF ENGINEER – MANXMAN

Dean's career at sea began in 1986 as an Engineer Cadet with Bibby Line, sailing on general cargo and tankers. He moved to Metcalfe Shipping Co. Ltd to work on drillship rig vessels, before joining the Steam Packet Company in 1991 as an Engineer on *Peveril* and *King Orry*. He was promoted to Chief Engineer in 2005, sailing on *Lady of Mann*, *Ben-my-Chree* and *Manannan*.

Dean gained a huge amount of knowledge and experience of the Company fleet over 30 years and assisted with *Manxman's* plan approvals and detail design, with a particular focus on engine room layouts, system design and machinery selection.

Dean and Andy rotated on site throughout the build period, but in the later stages worked together for the trials and testing of *Manxman* before taking command for the delivery voyage to the Isle of Man.

On arrival in Douglas *Manxman* undertook extensive life saving drills and tests. *(Miles Cowsill)*

A view of the bow thruster units on the starboard side of the ship. (*Steven Wilson*)

Crew working on **Manxman** have a covered area in the bow whilst undertaking mooring duties in port. (*Miles Cowsill*)

A view on Deck 10 of **Manxman** looking forward. (*Miles Cowsill*)

In the event of failure of the main bridge, **Manxman** has a second back-up bridge to enable her to continue to operate. *(Miles Cowsill)*

The spacious bridge of **Manxman**. *(Miles Cowsill)*

There are extensive facilities for officers and crew working on board for two weeks at a time. *(Miles Cowsill)*

The *Manxman* carries an a broad range of life saving equipment including two high speed rescue boats. *(Miles Cowsill)*

The upper deck allows coaches to unload with easy access next to the lifts. *(Miles Cowsill)*

A view of the main car deck. Wider turning areas and lanes makes for easier loading of freight. *(Miles Cowsill)*

The mezzanine deck on Deck 5 allows car traffic to load early on overnight sailings from Heysham. *(Miles Cowsill)*

As with the **Ben-my-Chree** there is an hydraulic ramp linking Deck 3 with Deck 5 *(Miles Cowsill)*

MANXMAN PRINCIPAL PARTICULARS

GENERAL

Hull No.	8311
Name of vessel	Manxman
Port of registry	Douglas
Nationality	Isle of Man
IMO No.	9917244
Call letters	MLHL7
Classification	LR
Type of ship	1,000 Persons Class Roll-On/Roll-Off and Passenger Ship
Keel laying date	24 December 2021

PRINCIPAL DIMENSIONS

Length - over all	133.25 m
Length - between perpendiculars	122.00 m
Breadth (moulded)	25.70 m
Breadth across belting	26.06 m
Depth (moulded) to No. 3 Deck (Main deck)	8.60 m
Depth (moulded) to No. 5 Deck (Upper deck)	14.70 m
Design draft (moulded)	5.20 m
Maximum summer load draft (moulded)	5.60 m
Scantling draft (moulded)	5.80 m
Keel thickness	11.00 mm
Maximum summer load draft (extreme)	5.611 m

LIGHTWEIGHT & DEADWEIGHT

Lightweight	9,387 tonnes
Deadweight	3,096 tonnes
Displacement	12,483 tonnes

COMPLEMENT

Passengers	949	Crew	51

PROPELLING MACHINERY

Propulsion system	Electric Propulsion Motor
Main generator engines	2 x Wärtsilä 10V31 + 2 x Wärtsilä 8V31
Maximum propulsion power (MPP)	2 x 7,850kW propulsion systems
Service propulsion power (SPP)	2 x 6,070kW propulsion systems
Propellor (2 sets)	4 x Nickel Aluminium Bronze 4,300 mm controllable pitch propellers
Design speed	19.25knots (at SPP without sea margin)

8

DELIVERY
VOYAGE

Senior Master Andy Atkinson was responsible for delivering *Manxman* from Ulsan to the Isle of Man and presents a detailed log of this epic voyage.

SATURDAY 13TH MAY 2023

The *Manxman* departed Hyundai Mipo Dockyard, Ulsan, Korea at 14:52 (06:52 in the Isle of Man), a little ahead of the 15:00 scheduled departure. The pilot disembarked at 15:32 and at 15:50 we were Full Away on the sea passage to Singapore, our first stop on the way home. Immediately after clearing Ulsan, we passed between the Korean city of Busan, and the Japanese island of Tsushima and continued to head south through the Korea Strait. By midnight, the ship had completed the first 136 miles of the trip home.

SUNDAY 14TH MAY

A warm and sunny day at sea in the East China Sea opened between the Korean island of Jeju and the southern islands of Japan. By midday we passed 200 miles east of Shanghai, and the mouth of the Yangtze River. Overall, we sailed 405 miles throughout the day.

The *Manxman* moves away from the quay at Ulsan as she heads home on her 12,241 nautical mile journey to Douglas. *(Andy Atkinson)*

MONDAY 15TH MAY

At midday we entered the Taiwan Strait between Taiwan and mainland China, which separates the East and South China seas. It's about as wide as twice the distance from Heysham to Douglas. Today we covered 401 miles.

A once in a lifetime opportunity. The *Manxman*'s delivery crew assemble for the camera. *(Andy Atkinson)*

TUESDAY 16TH MAY

Routine inspections found some slight fuel contamination. Safety is our first priority, so as a precaution we diverted towards Hong Kong to collect spare parts. We spent the day in a holding position until we had the appropriate clearances from the Hong Kong authorities for our entry. As Hong Kong is an hour behind Korea, we put our clocks back today. We will do this seven more times on our way back home.

WEDNESDAY 17TH MAY

Today we entered Hong Kong for our fuel and stores. At 17:30 we anchored off the southeast of Lamma Island. Bunkering fuel went well and by midnight we were preparing to depart.

THURSDAY 18TH MAY

Our anchor was aweigh just after midnight, and we headed south resuming our voyage to Singapore. We're now in the tropics and it's so warm that just before midnight the fire alarm went off. All Steam Packet crew are trained in firefighting for the safety of our passengers, but luckily it was a false alarm. By the time the crew not on watch went back to bed at midnight we had covered a further 361 miles.

FRIDAY 19TH MAY

Heading south, we passed the Paracel Islands in the South China Sea. These are known as the Chinese Maldives! The traffic's getting busy; there are lots of fishing boats offshore, as well as the heavy shipping traffic between China and Singapore and Indonesia. Today we sailed 373 miles.

SATURDAY 20TH MAY

During the morning we passed 160 miles off the Mekong River delta, and as the day progressed moved further south until we were east of the Gulf of Thailand. The weather has been overcast, with light winds, thunderstorms, and occasionally rainy squalls. During the day we covered 382 miles.

SUNDAY 21ST MAY

This evening we arrived at the port of Singapore - the world's second-busiest port, and the biggest ship refuelling centre. We'll take a short break here to assess the ship's systems after a good shakedown at sea on the voyage so far. Before we leave port, we'll also take on additional fuel for the next leg of the voyage, to Colombo, Sri Lanka.

SUNDAY 28TH MAY

Leaving Singapore, we heaved our anchor aweigh at 08:27. The pilot left by boat shortly after departure and we were on our way continuing our journey home west along

The morning sun catches **Manxman** with the Indonesian islands of Batam and Bintan south of Singapore in the background. *(Andy Atkinson)*

the Singapore Strait. After clearing the island, we passed the most southerly point of mainland Asia, Tanjung Piai, on the south coast of the Malay Peninsula. As we followed the Singapore Strait into the Strait of Malacca, most of the day was spent following a Traffic Separation Scheme. This is a routing requirement for ships which lays down a pre-determined lane for traffic in each direction – a bit like a road for ships. Closer to home, there's a Traffic Separation Scheme on the approaches to Liverpool. In the afternoon we passed the historic trading port of Malacca. By the end of the day the Straits were clearing, as we followed a route 40 miles off the east coast of Sumatra Island, Indonesia.

MONDAY 29TH MAY

Before we get to Colombo, we will gradually put our clocks back 2½ hours, so this morning we put them back one hour. On our way home we're following the Spice Routes, also known as the Maritime Silk Roads. They are

the most direct routes between the Far East and Europe by sea. It would take about a quarter of a million trips for *Manxman* to carry the amount of trade which flows between Asia and Europe each year. Just before midnight we passed south of the Nicobar Islands, and over the course of the day we have steamed 430 miles.

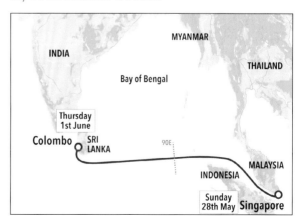

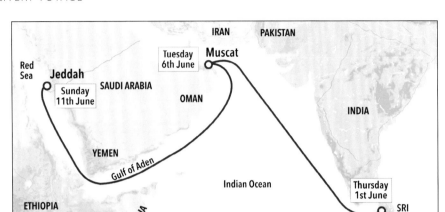

TUESDAY 30TH MAY

Our clocks went back again one hour this morning. As we crossed the Indian Ocean, just outside the Bay of Bengal, we hit a milestone on our way home at we crossed the 090°E meridian. Meridians of longitude run north to south, like the segments of an orange, and describe where in the world you are in east or west direction, relative to the Royal Observatory in Greenwich. 090°E means that we are east of London, and halfway between there and the International Date Line in the Pacific Ocean. Because they're shaped like orange segments, they don't tell us a lot about distance without also knowing our latitude, as they're wider apart at the equator and meet at the poles. On our way back we will cross the Greenwich meridian in the Mediterranean Sea and carry further on to about 9° 51'W, as we pass off the coast of Lisbon and head up the Atlantic towards the English Channel. Douglas's longitude is 004° 28'W.

WEDNESDAY 31ST MAY

We put our clocks back again by half an hour this morning. At around 04:00 ship's time (22:30 IoM time) *Manxman* was approximately 350-nm to the nearest point of land (halfway between Sri Lanka and Indonesia). With the

expected routes between each of the next ports this means that this was the furthest point from land that *Manxman* will be on the delivery voyage. It also means that given *Manxman's* expected future sailing schedule this would have been the furthest point from land that *Manxman* will ever be in the ship's lifetime.

THURSDAY 1ST JUNE

We reached Colombo today. The pilot boarded just after 08:00 and we were alongside made fast to the cruise berth by 09:12. This was just a quick stop for us to take stores and fuel for our onward journey, so we departed again at 19:00 towards Muscat, in Oman.

FRIDAY 2ND JUNE

At about 08:00 we passed approximately 20 miles off Cape Comorin (Kanyakumari), the most southerly tip of

Alongside in Colombo, Sri Lanka on 1st June. *(Andy Atkinson)*

The **Manxman** takes on fuel at Jeddah. (Andy Atkinson)

mainland India. At 22:30 we entered the Nine Degree Channel. Named because it passes across the 09°N parallel of latitude, separating Minicoy Island, and the rest of the Lakshadweep Islands. During today, we travelled 350 miles.

SATURDAY 3RD JUNE

We put our clocks back half an hour this morning, as Muscat is an hour and a half behind Colombo. As we left the Nine Degree Channel, we passed Southwest of the Indian Lakshadweep Islands which are in the Arabian Sea between the Maldives and mainland India. The name Lakshadweep means 'One hundred thousand islands', but our charts show that there aren't really that many. In the evening, the crew gathered in the mess to watch the start of the TT races – it's a shame to be away from it but we look forward to being part of it next year!

SUNDAY 4TH / MONDAY 5TH JUNE

Continuing to cross the Arabian Sea, these two days at sea were uneventful. We made landfall off Oman at about 22:00 and turned north on a slight dog's leg towards our next port call in Muscat, the capital of Oman.

TUESDAY 6TH JUNE

Today was another milestone as we reached the half-way point of our trip home. We visited Muscat, set within the stunning Hajar Mountains. At 07:16 we were at anchor off Mina Sultan Qaboos, which is the home of the Omani Royal Yacht Squadron and we even saw the Sultan's yacht sail. Our visit was just a quick one for fuel and stores and as soon as we had finished taking bunkers, we were keen to proceed on the second half of our trip home. Our leg to Jeddah, Saudi Arabia commenced at 17:06.

WEDNESDAY, 7TH JUNE

As the day opened, we rounded Ra's al-Hadd, the most easterly point of the Arabian Peninsula. As we approach the Gulf of Aden and the coast of Yemen, we held a security drill as this area has been designated a High-Risk Area by shipping industry authorities. The *Manxman* is a very secure ship - our speed and freeboard make us a very difficult target for criminals. Still, it was good for our crew to practise how to keep themselves and the ship safe and secure.

THURSDAY, 8TH JUNE

Early in the morning we passed the Khuriya Muriya Islands off the coast of Oman. In 1503, a squadron of Portuguese warships was wrecked here in bad weather. The officer in command of the squadron, Vicente Sodré was lost in the shipwrecks. This was just five years after Dom Vicente's nephew, Vasco de Gama, made history as the first European to sail to India. Thankfully *Manxman* was in very little danger of running aground as we passed 50 miles away from the islands. By the end of the day, we were about to enter the Gulf of Aden.

FRIDAY, 9TH JUNE

Half an hour after midnight, we passed 125 miles north of Cape Guardafui, on the peak of the Horn of Africa. Beaconing the entrance to the Gulf of Aden, the historical ports around this area were once major trading centres for spices, especially cinnamon, between ancient Europe and India. Ra's Fartak in Yemen marks the northern limit. Slowly, Cape Guardafui and Ra's Fartak get further apart each year due to an underwater ridge between the tectonic plates here. In the evening we passed about 50 miles south of Aden. Lesseps' construction of the Suez Canal in 1869 led to Aden becoming an important seaport. Yemen's coastline closed towards us afterwards as we turned

A rare photographic opportunity. The ***Manxman*** heads towards the spectacular Suez Canal bridge at Al Banhawo. *(Andy Atkinson)*

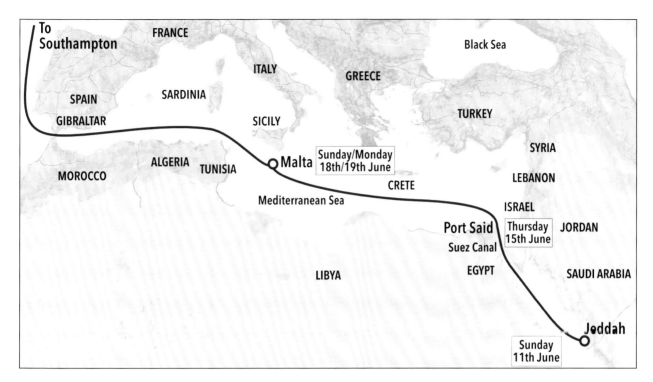

northwards towards the Bab El-Mandeb straits in the western limit of the Gulf of Aden.

SATURDAY, 10TH JUNE

A little after 08:00 this morning we passed through the Bab-El Mandeb straits which separate Yemen from Djibouti and Eritrea. We went through the large strait which led us only two miles south of Perim island. Once through, we were in the Red Sea. At 19:00 we passed about 20 miles off the Zubair islands of Yemen. One of these islands is fewer than ten years old, having only been formed in September 2013 by an undersea volcano!

SUNDAY, 11TH JUNE

We have been following the main route from the entrance to the Red Sea at the Bab El-Mandeb straits to the Suez Canal in Egypt. Before we get to Suez we will call into Saudi Arabia for fuel. Therefore, we turned off the through route and started making our way towards Jeddah. By 22:30 we were anchored. The anchorage here is very deep, so we had to use most of our anchor chain to keep us in position.

MONDAY, 12TH JUNE

Whilst at anchor off Jeddah we took stores and fuel, and offloaded garbage. We weighed our anchor at 19:10 and departed on our way again. Our next stop will be Malta, but we will pass through the Suez Canal on our way.

TUESDAY, 13TH JUNE

As the day opened, *Manxman* was in the Red Sea between Saudi Arabia and Sudan. Just before midday we passed the Daedalus Reef and its 1930s lighthouse. At

The *Manxman* pauses for fuel and supplies in Malta. *(Andy Atkinson)*

22:00, we entered the Gulf of Suez between Shaker Island and Sharm El-Sheikh.

WEDNESDAY, 14TH JUNE

This morning we arrived off Suez ready for the transit of the Canal. Today's convoy was slightly late leaving so, as we approached Suez, we were advised to slow down to allow the holding anchorage to clear. Once the day's convoy had departed, we were given an anchoring position to wait and anchored off Ras al-Masala at 10:15 as the rest of our convoy arrived. Later today various officials arrived for formalities. A Suez Canal Inspector boarded us to ensure that our ship meets the strict requirements of the Suez Canal Authority - this inspection wasn't a problem for *Manxman*; in less than an hour we were granted clearance to proceed on tomorrow's convoy.

THURSDAY, 15TH JUNE

During our transit of the Suez Canal, we took three different pilots. The first boarded us at 05:30 and took us just 4 miles from our anchorage position to the entrance of the Canal. We exchanged pilots at 06:45 and entered the Suez Canal. The Canal is 162 miles long and has no locks. Instead, the tidal effects of the Great Bitter Lake act as a natural lock, separating the sea level of the Mediterranean and Red Seas. We reached the Great Bitter Lake at about 10:00, and that was where we passed the southbound convoy heading the other way. At 12:30 we changed pilots again for the final stretch. At about 16:00, we exited the Canal near Port Said into the Levantine Sea and altered course towards Malta.

FRIDAY, 16TH JUNE

After the business of the Suez Canal yesterday, today was a quiet day. As the day opened, we were 40 miles north of the city of Rosetta on the Nile Delta. By 16:00, we were about half-way between the Greek island of Crete and Libya.

SATURDAY 17TH JUNE

As the day opened, we were about 90 miles south of Elafonisos Lighthouse off the south-west coast of Crete. At 02:00, we put our clocks back to match local time in Malta. We are now only one hour ahead of the Isle of Man. While those at home have been enjoying the heat wave, we've found the weather noticeably cooler in the Mediterranean than it was. This has been supplemented by the Mistral, a Mediterranean wind from the northwest has been blowing cool air from Europe towards us. As the day went on, we crossed the Mediterranean south of the Ionian Sea, and by midnight we were about 120 miles southeast of Portopalo on the south-eastern tip of Sicily.

SUNDAY 18TH JUNE

We arrived in Malta today, picking up the pilot at 07:48, and by 08:25 we were tied up alongside in Birżebbuġa on the southeast coast of Malta. This is not the first time a *Manxman* has visited Malta. The first *Manxman* was requisitioned by the Admiralty during the Great War and saw service as a seaplane carrier as *HMS Manxman* before returning to the Irish Sea in 1920 under the ownership of the Steam Packet. Frank Mason's painting 'HMS Manxman Refitting in French Creek, Malta before leaving for Ismid' documents her time here while she formed part of the Eastern Mediterranean Fleet. During the Second World War, *Manxman* was again requisitioned by the Royal Navy but this time renamed *HMS Caduceus*, because by the war's start the Royal Navy had ordered a minelayer to be built which they named *HMS Manxman*. The first *Manxman*, as *HMS Caduceus*, was involved in Operation Dynamo, the 1940 allied evacuation from Dunkirk, and never returned to passenger service. Once alongside we took fuel, provisions, and water for the next part of our journey. We also welcomed 27 crewmembers who joined and started familiarising themselves with the new ship.

MONDAY 19TH JUNE

To continue the familiarisation of our new crew, we held an emergency drill. This enabled us to practice how we will keep each other safe at sea. Once we were happy that our crew understood their emergency duties, we prepared to leave. The pilot boarded shortly before midday, and we cast off our mooring lines at 12:15. Malta is our last scheduled stop before we reach British waters.

Malta is another milestone for the journey because it is on roughly the same latitude as Ulsan. From here to the Isle of Man, *Manxman* will nearly always be reaching new heights further north. Our first course took us round the north coast of Malta and from there through the strait of

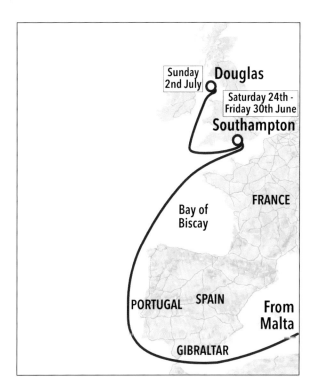

Sicily and by midnight we were north of Cap Bon in Tunisia.

TUESDAY 20TH JUNE

Starting the day around 15 miles north of Tunisia, we followed the North African coast past Algeria. The coast of the Maghreb was, in the 16th Century, notorious for the Corsairs. We're pleased that these days it's much safer and we were in very little risk of being kidnapped into slavery!

In the evening we took advantage of the good weather and held a crew barbecue.

WEDNESDAY 21ST JUNE

We put our clocks back for the final time to match the Isle of Man. Coincidentally, at 25 hours long it was one of the longest days for us this year on the Northern

Welcome to Britain! The *Manxman* passes Hythe Pier as she sails up Southampton Water on Saturday 24th June 2023. *(John Bryant)*

Hemisphere's summer solstice. In the evening we passed through the Straits of Gibraltar which separate the Atlantic Ocean from the Mediterranean Sea. On an otherwise clear day, cloud at the peak of Jebel Musa, the southern Pillar, was formed by orographic lift as surface air gets forced upwards into an area of lower pressure and therefore cools.

THURSDAY 22ND JUNE

As the day opened, we were 40 miles west of Cape Trafalgar, where Admirals Nelson and Collingwood won victory in 1805 over the French and Spanish Navies. By about 06:00 we were approaching Cape St Vincent and, as we continued along the Portuguese coast, we passed off Lisbon at 12:30. At 009° 51'.4W we expect this to be the furthest west the ship will ever be during her life in service. By midnight we were approaching Cape Finisterre.

FRIDAY 23RD JUNE

At 00:30 we passed 23-miles off Cape Finisterre on the north-western coast of Spain. By midnight we had reached its namesake, the French department Finistère in Brittany. These two edges of the Bay of Biscay were both named by the Romans who named them *Finis Terrae*, the Edge of the World.

SATURDAY 24TH JUNE

Opening the day off Cherbourg in France, we proceeded up the English Channel as we approached Southampton. We met the pilot near the Nab Tower off Portsmouth in the Eastern Solent and proceeded between the Isle of Wight and the Hampshire coast, before turning into Southampton Water around the Brambles Bank. We moored at about 15:00 at 104 Berth in Southampton. We

A warm welcome home! The *Manxman* arrives at Douglas after her epic trip from Korea. *(Barry Edwards)*

will have some final work done here to prepare the ship for our arrival home in Douglas.

FRIDAY 30TH JUNE

With all work completed on board, *Manxman* left her berth in Southampton at 20:55 under the command of Capt. Jonathan Palmer to begin the final leg of our homeward journey. We made our way down the Solent and headed east past Portsmouth before dropping off our pilot at the Nab Tower. We then set course around the south of the Isle of Wight and down the English Channel.

SATURDAY IST JULY

Manxman continued her journey westwards, sailing parallel to the south coast of England before turning

sharply to the north as we rounded Land's End at around 12:30. Steady progress continued as we headed up the Irish Sea, running along the Welsh coast to pass around Anglesey and steer a course for the Isle of Man.

SUNDAY 2ND JULY

With the Isle of Man on the radar at last, we exchanged whistles as we passed the *Ben-my-Chree*, and headed into Douglas Harbour, arriving on our berth on schedule at 09:00. It was gratifying to see so many people gathered on Douglas Head to witness our historic arrival on a lovely Manx morning. Home at last after an epic and unforgettable voyage.

ACKNOWLEDGEMENTS

The level of enthusiasm for the *Manxman* project has been reflected in the wholesome support given to the authors in the compilation of this volume.

The leader of the Isle of Man government, Chief Minister Hon Alfred Cannan MHK, provided valuable insight into government motivation for the project.

Peter Corrin and John Hendy were kind enough to record their personal experience and the historical record of previous *Manxman* vessels in the Steam Packet fleet.

Steam Packet Chairman Lars Ugland gave freely of his time to describe the background to the project and kindly provided the Foreword to this book. Managing Director Brian Thomson was supportive to the publication throughout and contributed the Introduction chapter. Fleet Manager Jim Royston spent significant time amidst his busy schedule assisting with many aspects of the book and gave a valuable insight into the engineering aspects of the build. Senior Master Andy Atkinson provided a log of the journey from Ulsan to the UK and shared his enthusiasm for the operational aspects of the new build. Customer Services Manager Seamus Byrne looked forward to the vessel's introduction to service with details of the quality on board services to be offered.

For Houlder Ltd, David Wing helped with background to the outline design of *Manxman* and technical aspects underpinning the ship's general arrangement. At SMC Design, Matt Fyvie, Liam Kirk, Emmie Ratter, Liz Richardson, and Alun Roberts shared their passion for the interior design of the *Manxman*. Emmie Ratter also provided introductions to the artists whose work is featured on the vessel. The selected artists - Ellie Baker, Adam Berry, Sally Black,

Amy Bourbon, Jade Boylan, Bruno Cavellic, Anna Cloucas, Ian Coulson, Megan Hindley, Darren Jackson, Andrew Mackellar, Jacqui Mulvagh, Stephanie Quayle, Graham Rider, and Ron Strathdee - illustrated the depth of talent amongst the Manx artists community and were each interviewed to share their enthusiasm for the commissioned works.

Ryan Choi, Senior Manager of the Contract Management Department at Hyundai MIPO, provided technical data, statistics, and a helpful outline of the work of the shipyard. Minseok Jang, President of Sejin Technical Industries Co. Ltd, helped with information on the work undertaken by his company in providing the high-quality outfitting of the vessel. Ole Martin Sletten provided details and specification of the BazePort infotainment system fitted on *Manxman*, whilst Argo Sildvee helpfully assisted with information on the extensive work undertaken by the Estonian Marine and Manufacturing Initiative. Paul Grace, Principal Surveyor at Isle of Man Ship Registry, outlined the work needed at Douglas harbour to accommodate the arrival of *Manxman*. Barry Edwards, Isle of Man correspondent for *Ferry & Cruise Review* magazine, helped proof read the text and photographed *Manxman*'s arrival in the Island.